REMAINS

Historical and Literary

CONNECTED WITH THE PALATINE COUNTIES OF

Lancaster and Chester

VOLUME XXIII—THIRD SERIES

MANCHESTER:

Printed for the Chetham Society

1976

This volume is published in association with the Bradford University Press. The Chetham Society is grateful for its generous support in this venture

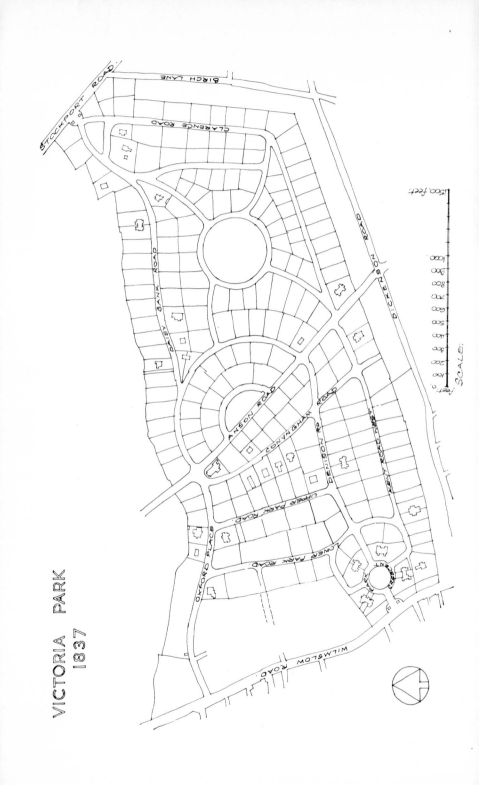

VICTORIA PARK
1837

SCALE:

VICTORIA PARK
MANCHESTER:
A NINETEENTH-CENTURY SUBURB IN ITS SOCIAL AND ADMINISTRATIVE CONTEXT

by

MAURICE SPIERS

MANCHESTER
Printed for the Chetham Society
1976

PRINTED IN GREAT BRITAIN
BY BUTLER AND TANNER LTD, FROME AND LONDON

PREFACE

The thesis on which this book is based was started out of curiosity. At that time it seemed odd that a comparatively large area, more or less at the centre of the conurbation of Manchester, could remain 'private', go on levying 'tolls', and have its roads in a more or less permanent state of disrepair as late as 1954. After a few inquiries, I discovered that the Corporation of Manchester had 'taken over' what had been for a century a private park which had been 'governed' by a committee of its inhabitants. At this stage it seemed probable that this subject matter could be interpreted as a special aspect of local government, and this idea received added encouragement when it was realized that the 'life' of the Park began just before the incorporation of the city in 1838. A historical treatment, therefore, could very probably be conveniently 'phased' along with the development of local government institutions. The final decision to adopt this framework was taken when it was discovered that the minute books of the 'governing body', the Victoria Park Trust Committee, existed from 1896 to 1954 and that the minute books of the Rusholme Local Board of Health, applying to the surrounding township before it became part of Manchester, were deposited in the Central Library. In addition, the solicitors who dealt with the take-over in 1954 had collected detailed material concerning certain important aspects of internal administration, which they were able to allow me to consult.

In order to give a social context to this chiefly administrative history, I included two chapters which attempt to describe what sort of an area the Park was at various stages of its history. I have attempted to identify the contemporary historical context by describing where possible some of the social and political activities of leading residents, and when high-income residence began to be less characteristic, by describing the uses to which the property was put.

This material is contained in two chapters. The introduction takes the story down to about 1860, and chapter 5 to 1940. This sketch of the social history of the area has revealed that it is very probable that the Park has passed through three fairly distinct phases of occupation. The first, the occupation by the merchant class, corresponded to an economic dominance of medium-sized capitalist enterprise. The second, the arrival of the professional men after about 1875, possibly indicated the emergence of a more professionally oriented society, and the third, the dominance of service institutions, corresponded to the emergence of the welfare state.

The remaining chapters deal with a factual account of the internal administration of the Park, and its relations with local government. Chapter 1 describes the origin of the scheme, and the formation of the Trust Committee. Chapter 2 describes the relations of this Committee with the Local Board of Health, and chapter 3, the response of the Park Committee to the incorporation of the surrounding township in the City of Manchester. Chapter 4 describes the attempts of the Committee to resist the coming of modern grid-iron housing and the breaking of the so-called 'building tie', and chapters 6 and 7, how the Park was first able to resist the passage of public transport in 1902, but after 1920 was forced to accept the passage of trams, and finally, how in 1939 the area was cut in two by the opening of one of its main roads to free traffic. Chapter 8 describes the final years after the second world war and the negotiations for the take-over by the Corporation, while a short concluding chapter deals with the recent declaration of the Park as a Conservation Area and briefly sketches the contemporary situation.

CONTENTS

ACKNOWLEDGMENTS

The publication of this book has been a co-operative effort, and the author owes thanks to friends and colleagues. When much of the material was originally collected, Professor W. J. M. Mackenzie, who exercised such a creative influence on social science in Manchester, was particularly encouraging. At that time, too, the staff of the Local History Section of the Central Reference Library were extremely helpful.

In the process of revision, Dr. W. H. Chaloner gave me the benefit of his intimate knowledge of Manchester's social and economic history, and in his capacity as a member of Council of the Chetham Society kindly gave time for consultation on the availability of that body's generous support. I am especially indebted to the Bradford University Press Committee, its Chairman, Professor A. H. Bottomley, and the Director of the Press, F. Earnshaw, A. L. A., Librarian of Bradford University, for their generosity and flexibility in supporting this co-operative publication venture.

Finally, I owe a debt of gratitude to the planning department of the Manchester Corporation, who provided up-to-date information, and to Mr. Peter Helm of the Rusholme and Fallowfield Preservation Society, who made available photographs from private sources and prepared them for publication. He also gave time to prepare the appendix on residents, which I am sure greatly adds to the interest of the book.

MAURICE SPIERS

LIST OF ILLUSTRATIONS

Erratum

The illustrations on Plates 8 and 9 have inadvertently been transposed. Plate 8 in fact shows Regent House/ Marylands and Plate 9 Ivy Villa, the south side.

SOURCES

General

1. Anon [Dr. E. Bosdin-Leech], *A Short Account of the Victoria Park, Manchester*, Manchester, 1937. Published by the Park Trust Committee in Commemoration of the Centenary of the opening of the Park on 31st July 1837. This is a very brief outline history.
2. The Bosdin Leech MSS. Dr. Bosdin Leech wrote the Centenary History. The material that he gathered was preserved and passed to the Corporation in 1954 and is no longer in the Local History library in St. Peter's Square. They contain all agreements made by the Trust Committee, all briefs and opinions as to the legal status of the Trust Committee, copies of extracts from early minute books of the Trust Committee, some letters of Committee members, the Committee minute books 1896–1954, and other miscellaneous maps and papers.
3. The Poor Law Rate Books of the Township of Rusholme, 1834–1895. The rate was assessed annually, and sometimes bi-annually. Every property owner, occupier, estimated rent, and rateable value is written out. In some cases the actual date of occupation is given. These books were used to establish length of occupation of various residents, and the dates of house building because of greater accuracy.
4. The Minutes of the Rusholme Local Board of Health, 1848–85. Provided most of the material for chapter 2; are contained in ten bound volumes in the Local History Library.
5. *Manchester City Council Proceedings*, 1879–85.
6. Biographical, and newspaper cutting files at the Local History Library were invaluable for access to information on particular individuals and areas of the city.

Particular

The above main sources provided most of the material for the thesis, especially those chapters concerned with the detailed negotiations. Individual residents were traced through obituaries as footnoted in the text. The following is an alphabetical list of all other sources:

Ashworth, W.   *The Genesis of Modern British Town Planning*, 1954
Axon, W. E. A.   *The Annals of Manchester*, 1886
Bergel, E. E.   *Urban Sociology*, 1965
Boase, F.   *Modern English Biography*, 6 vols. 1965 reprint

Brazil, Angela. *My Own School Days*, n.d. (1925)

Briggs, A. *History of Birmingham, volume II: Borough and City, 1865–1938*, 1952

Bryce, James. *Report of the Schools Enquiry Commission*, 1864–67.

Buckley, J. S. *The History of Birch-in-Rusholme*, Manchester, 1910.

Burstall, Sara A. *The Story of the Manchester High School for Girls, 1871–1911*, Manchester, 1911

Cardus, Neville. *Second Innings*, 1950

Chorley, Katherine C. *Manchester Made Them*, 1950

Crofton, H. T. *Old Moss Side*, Manchester, 1903

Dickens, A. L. *Report to the General Board of Health on a further inquiry at Rusholme*, 1855

Farnie, D. A. 'The English Cotton Industry 1850–1896', typescript; M.A. thesis, Manchester University, 1953

Freeman, T. W. *The Conurbations of Great Britain*, 2nd rev. ed. 1966

Green, L. P. *Provincial Metropolis: the future of local government in south-east Lancashire*, 1959

Grindon, L. H. *Manchester Banks and Bankers*, 2nd ed. 1878

Hayes, L. M. *Reminiscences of Manchester and of some of its local surroundings from 1840*, 1904

Hopkinson, Sir Alfred. *Penultima*, 1930

——— *Rebuilding Britain*, 1918

Hurst, Sir Gerald B., *Closed Chapters*, 1942.

Lawrenson, T. E., *Hall of Residence: St. Anselm's Hall . . . 1907–1957*, 1957

McConechy, J. S. 'The economic value of the Ship Canal to Manchester and district', *Trans. Manchester Statistical Society*, Session 1912–13, pp. 1–126

McCord, N. *The Anti-Corn Law League, 1838–1846*, 1958

Mills, W. Haslam. *Sir Charles W. Macara, Bart.; a study of modern Lancashire*, 2nd ed. Manchester, 1917

Mumford, A. A. *The Manchester Grammar School, 1515–1919*, Manchester, 1919

[Nicklin, Rev. T.], *Hulme Hall, Manchester, 1881*, 1930 (unreliable)

Prentice, A. *History of the Anti-Corn-Law League*, 2 vols., 1853, reprinted 1968

——— *Historical Sketches and Personal Recollections of Manchester . . . 1792 to 1832*, 1851, 3rd ed. 1970

Rawlinson, Sir Robert. *Report to the General Board of Health on a preliminary inquiry into the sewerage, drainage, and the sanitary condition of the inhabitants of Rusholme*, 1850

Rawson, H. (ed.). *An Historical Record of some recent enterprises of the Corporation of Manchester and of its co-operation in the completion of the Manchester Ship Canal*, Manchester, 1894

Redford, A., assisted by Ina S. Russell. *The History of Local Government in Manchester*, 3 vols., 1939–40

Rees, H. 'A growth map for the Manchester Region', *Economic Geography*, Worcester, Mass., vol. 23, 1947, pp. 136–42

Roscoe, Sir H. E. *The Life and Experiences of Sir Henry Enfield Roscoe . . . written by himself*, 1906

Royle, W. *Rusholme: past and present*, Manchester, 1905

Scholes, J. 'Manchester Foreign Merchants, 1784–1870' (MS. in Manchester Public Library)

Stewart, C. *The Stones of Manchester*, 1956

Sutherland, G. A. *Dalton Hall: a Quaker Venture*, 1963

Thompson, J. *The Owens College: its Foundation and Growth*, Manchester, 1886

Whitaker, P. 'The Growth of Liberal Organisations in Manchester from the 1860s to 1903', typescript; Ph.D. thesis, Manchester University, 1956

Wilkinson, W. C. *Sketches of Fallowfield*, 1888

Newspapers

Manchester Courier. 4.4.1836 for the Victoria Park Company prospectus

—— 4.6.1836 for Brighton Grove Scheme Prospectus

Manchester City News. 1. and 10.9.1900 for articles on the history of Greenheys

South Manchester Gazette. 9.5.1885, 16.5.1885 for references to negotiations for the incorporation of Rusholme. This newspaper was published for three years only, 1885–88.

See also a small file of newspaper cuttings on Victoria Park in Local History Library for general press references.

INTRODUCTION

SOCIAL, POLITICAL AND ECONOMIC BACKGROUND, 1820–1860

Although this book is concerned with some special aspects of Manchester local government, it is necessary for a more complete understanding to place the 'phenomenon' of Victoria Park in various contexts. These are,

(i) The rapid expansion of mercantile Manchester and the emergence of a new social class demanding local and later national political and social expression.
(ii) The contemporary conception of building for investment or speculation.
(iii) The condition of local government regulation of what are now considered public matters.

Johnson's map of Manchester and the surrounding districts in 1820 shows that the townships of Hulme, Moss Side, Chorlton Row, Ardwick, Newton Heath and Cheetham were all largely rural in aspect and economic activity. However, in the centre of the town, the process of expansion was beginning, showing itself as the replacement of merchants' houses by warehouses during the middle and late 1820s. An article[1] about the Barbour family, which describes the early life of Robert Barbour,[2] mentioning his partnership with a fellow Scot, says, 'John Macfarlane, a sagacious Scotchman, converted buildings just behind the Albion Hotel, to the amazement of the old townspeople.' The new warehouses spread into the surrounding streets, sometimes into open countryside, and sometimes alongside 'mean and wretched hovels'.[3] Merchants and manufacturers still lived in these central parts of the town, warehouses, slums and residences standing cheek by jowl. High Street was still considered as a residential quarter, for 'the commercial area [of the town] . . . prior to 1827 did not reach to a greater distance on the Infirmary side than High Street and the immediate neighbourhood of Spring Gardens'.[4] The extension of the commercial area of the town was accompanied by an extension of the suburbs. 'Since 1821 the town had been increasing rapidly, and now new avenues to the suburban parts were loudly called for.'[5] The Bury New Road, for example,

---

[1] *City News*, 5th May 1915. [2] See p. 7.
[3] See Grindon, *Manchester Banks and Bankers*, ch. 13, for detailed account of this expansion and p. 144.
[4] *ibid.*, p. 141. [5] *ibid.*, p. 137.

'extending from the corner of Broughton Lane, up the hill to Kersal and through Prestwich to Besses o' th' Barn', was opened on 19th October 1831.[1] The same year saw the beginning of work on the Stretford new road, which was completed 10th September 1832, and celebrated 'by a grand cavalcade . . . with music and banners'. To the south of the city, the suburbs of Ardwick, Chorlton Row and Hulme were already becoming the favoured retreats of some of the more enterprising of the commercial population. The 1820 map shows little building along Plymouth Grove. Slater's *Directory* for 1836 shows thirty-seven different occupiers under this street name, including some who later moved to Victoria Park. These were H. Salomons, W. R. Callender and John Leisler. Nelson Street, which cuts across from Oxford Street to Plymouth Grove, housed three merchants and five manufacturers, though there were some houses there in 1820. This region, stretching across some mile and a half from the town centre and taking in Ardwick Polygon, represented the southern limit of the out-of-town residence area. Greenheys, later to be built up and to form the chief centre of the German community, remained substantially underdeveloped in 1820,[2] and of course, there was still much land unbuilt upon, stretching into the city to the north of Ardwick and stretching into the city fronting Oxford Road.

During the early and middle 1830s, the out-of-town villa residence was just beginning to become fashionable. There remain, even today, many examples of this type of property that were put up between about 1835 and 1850. The broad band of country from Greenheys, Chorlton-on-Medlock, the northern parts of Rusholme (i.e. Victoria Park), Plymouth Grove and parts of Longsight and Ardwick contain examples of late Georgian terraces[3] and villa residences.[4] These houses were all occupied by the emerging mercantile class of the city.

Before the coming of the joint stock company house-building probably provided one of the most secure forms of private investment for the mercantile *nouveau-riche*. It gave a good return during prosperous times and a comparatively easily maintained reserve in bad times. Such building could, of course, take place on a variety of scales. At one level, a merchant would rent a property while making the beginnings of his fortune and then put up property for his own residence, perhaps with one or two other houses close by. At the other end of the scale, there was the tradition of town im-

---

[1] See Grindon, *Manchester Banks and Bankers*, pp. 138–9.

[2] 'The first house was put up in 1817 by John Kaye, a cabinet maker, who bought a piece of land, and put up the first villa,' (T. Swindells, *Manchester City News*, 1st, 10th September, 1900).

[3] The houses marked 'Chatsworth Terrace', map 1, remain at the corner of Nelson Street and Plymouth Grove.

[4] There are two such houses, close to the University at the corner of Dover Street, and opposite Nelson Street along Oxford Road.

provement through private estate development.[1] The Park promoters must clearly have conceived themselves as operating in such
a tradition. The tradition demanded privacy, internal rules, the exclusion of certain persons or types of activity, and planned ornamental development. Thus Ashworth writes of the Bedford Estate,
begun in 1774:

> Twenty acres were first laid out as gardens for the use of lessees, the
> intention being that buildings should be grouped around greens scattered
> over the whole area. Considerable restrictions were imposed on lessees. . . .
> No lessee was allowed to put up any sign, or to use a house as a shop or
> restaurant; the entrances were closed by gates and persons with no business
> in Bloomsbury were not admitted[2]

About this time, that is the middle 1830s, schemes larger than the
comparatively small, piece-by-piece schemes promoted by men like
Kaye,[3] but much smaller than the late eighteenth-century London
precedents described by Ashworth, were being projected around the
city of Manchester. If more than one speculator had an interest in
a particular piece of land, it would be natural to form a company.
One such scheme was promoted in Brighton Grove in 1834, but
failed some years later. Royle's *History of Birch-in-Rusholme*[4] gives a
very short account, mentioning that 'a private company was formed
to build some substantial houses and pleasure gardens on three sides
of a quadrangle . . . There was a lodge for entrance and another
for exit, and these stand today'. Royle includes an engraving 'of
the palatial residences, showing Birch Brook . . . running through
the grounds, . . . there being rustic bridges and terraces. . . .'[5]

It was possibly more typical for a speculator to take up a parcel
of land, lay out roads, and then advertise plots for building or let-
ting. Whalley Range is an example of this type of development.
Samuel Brooks, a banker, built Whalley House in 1834, and also
bought lands on the south side of Upper Chorlton Road, which
belonged to a farm situated close to the site of the present Whalley
Hotel.

In 1834, Brooks arranged to improve an old farm road which skirted
this farm to the north. This he called Upper Chorlton Road, to distinguish

[1] Ashworth, *The Genesis of Modern British Town Planning*, 1954, pp. 36–8.
[2] *Ibid.*, p. 36.
[3] 'Mr Kaye built most of the houses standing [in Greenheys] in 1838, borrowing
£50,000 from Miss Byrom' (T. Swindells, *ibid.*)
[4] Royle, 1914, pp. 30, 33.
[5] Actually, the Victoria Park Scheme was advertised formally before the
Brighton Grove Scheme. The prospectus of Brighton Grove Villas appeared on
4th June 1836. It comprised a similar exhortation to purchase property convenient
to both town and country, and then, 'Recently . . . it has been proposed in part to
supply that deficiency by the Victoria Park Tontine, which however good, can
only furnish a small portion of the accommodation so imperiously called for'
(*Manchester Courier*, 4th June 1836).

it from Chorlton Road, which had also been formed under his auspices, from Brook's Bar to Stretford Road, which had only just been formed. Both Chorlton Road and Upper Chorlton Road were barred by gates at the (hence the name) Brook's Bar end.[1]

There is very little information concerning how the estate was originally conceived, but it is certain that its development lay within the eighteenth-century tradition that Ashworth shows can be traced in London. Crofton writes: 'Mr. Samuel Brooks, when laying out Whalley Range, was greatly helped by John Shaw,[2] of Bowdon, who was a landscape gardener of great renown'.

It was not until the Public Health Act of 1848 that the Local Boards of Health were empowered to pay attention to the state of the roads, sewers, etc. There was the long tradition of private road ownership and private sewering. If an estate of any size was envisaged, the promoters therefore scored well if they could attract would-be tenants or buildings with the added advantage of an already laid-out road system, with some sort of main drainage.

In addition to Manchester, similar ventures were occurring in other parts of the country. For example, at Cressington Park, Liverpool, in 1851,

about 40 acres of land were purchased, and sold off in 174 plots. . . . The plots having been sold, there remained vested in the original owners, O'Kell and Jeffries, the roads, and a promenade along the sea wall. The object of the Deed was to declare trust concerning the roads and the promenade for the benefit of the purchasers and to provide for the payment of the necessary expenses, proportionately, by the owners. . . . The Deed contained elaborate provisions for the owners of the plot to meet and to decide what was an appropriate sum to be paid annually. . . .[3]

Similarly, Asa Briggs, in his *History of Birmingham*, mentions that in 1878[4] 'Widney Manor and Dorridge Park Estates, belonging to G. F. Muntz, were laid out for the building of villa residences, and the Great Western Railway arranged special express trains'[5] to Birmingham and Paddington.

The position that emerges, then, is that Victoria Park was a rather elaborate example of planned private building. Other less ambitious schemes were being projected locally, and there is some evidence that this local development formed part of a larger national develop-

---

[1] H. T. Crofton, *Old Moss Side*, p. 32.

[2] See biographical note of Shaw's son, *Manchester Faces and Places*, January 1901, p. 15. For the development of Bowdon as an opulent middle-class suburb, see H. Taine, *Taine's Notes on England*, ed. and trans. E. Hyams, 1957, p. 220 (where Victoria Park is also described without being precisely identified) and chapter VI ('From Bowdon to Ancoats'), in J. Rendel Harris (ed.) *The Life of Francis William Crossley*, 1899.

[3] See *Halsall and Others* v. *Brizell and Others*, 1957 *Chancery*, p. 169 (29th November 1956).

[4] A. Briggs, *History of Birmingham*, Vol. 11, p. 140.

[5] *Birmingham Post*, 23rd May 1878.

ment, at least in the emerging industrial cities. The building of the Park was made possible by the rapid expansion of Manchester during the late 1820s and early 1830s. The demand among the mercantile and manufacturing class for villa residences, and larger terraced property[1] was great, and the great outward expansion into Cheshire had begun.

Politically, of course, Victoria Park, especially that part which was first built up, lying towards the Wilmslow Road end, can be identified through its residents with the two great contemporary movements, i.e. the demand for the incorporation of the borough, and the movement for the repeal of the Corn Laws. Indeed, these two were, for the most part, political manifestations, springing from a common source; the growth of a wealthy social and economic class. The great stone houses demonstrated their arrival socially, incorporation in 1838 and the repeal of the Corn Laws in 1846 demonstrated it politically.[2]

Turning to personalities, it is possible to trace most of those who were closely connected with the Park's promotion and many early residents, with both the movement for incorporation, and the activities of the League. Of the promoters of the Victoria Park scheme, three were associated with the earliest years of the League. Joseph Adshead was a member of the 1839 League Council.[3] Thomas Harbottle, who incidentally had suffered the destruction of his factory in Portland Street at the hands of rioters in 1829, was a member of the 1839 Provisional Committee.[4] R. Bunting also is recorded as a member of this committee. As McCord points out, membership of this committee could mean only 'sympathy' and not necessarily activity.[5] The formation of the League Council in January 1839 shows how closely League and Park 'personnel' were connected. Those already mentioned, as well as James Kershaw (see p. 6) and other prominent persons such as George Hadfield (see p. 6), can be traced. The finance committee, for example, of nine persons contained four who were Park promoters or later residents.[6]

The typical pattern seems to have been that these notables of the late 1830s and early 1840s were, for the most part, immigrants, some from humble origins, others not so humble. William Romaine Callender, sen.[7] (d. 1872) for example, came to Manchester about 1815

---

[1] For example, terraces dating from late 1830s and early 1840s exist along Lloyd Street, Ducie Street and Cecil Street.

[2] Oddly enough the identity is almost complete. The first phase of the Park's life, before the Trust Committee came into existence, ended in 1846, and the last stone villa to be built was Langdale Hall, which was completed in 1847.

[3] Prentice, *Anti-Corn-Law League*, Vol. I, p. 105.

[4] Prentice, *Personal Recollections*, p. 347; *Anti-Corn-Law League*, vol. I, p. 105.

[5] McCord, *Anti-Corn-Law League*, p. 35.

[6] Prentice, *Anti-Corn-Law League*, Vol. I, p. 106.

[7] Whitaker, thesis, p. 26; Axon, *Annals*, p. 332; *Manchester Guardian*, 24th May 1872.

as a draper's assistant. After working as a salesman, he entered into partnership, and later formed the firm of Callender and Sons. He was closely associated with the incorporation movement, and the election of Poulett Thomson in 1832. Until about 1846 to 1847 he was a member of the Manchester Reform Association, but after the adoption of Bright as candidate, he took little further interest in politics. He lived in Victoria Park from 1845 to 1864. Whitaker refers to him as 'one of the Directors of the League, and a thoroughgoing Cobdenite'. He was one of the first aldermen of the City.

Probably typical of the successful professional immigrant of these expansionist years was George Hadfield, attorney.[1] He came from a Glossop family, but was born in Sheffield in 1787. He began to practise in Manchester in 1810, and was closely connected with the transfer of property in South Manchester during the 1820s and 1830s. He was one of the founders of the League, and had seconded the nomination of Poulett Thomson. He was a liberal of the old school, 'holding to the last, principles which were later abandoned by many, contending for purely voluntary effort, and universal religious teaching'. He was a leading spirit in the Lancashire Congregational Union, attending Rusholme Road Chapel with George Wilson about this time. Retiring from his profession, he was M.P. for Sheffield, 1852–74. He lived in the Park from 1838 until his death in 1879.[2]

The purpose of these brief biographical notes is to give some guide to the social and political 'setting' of the Park. Perhaps the most typical[3] of all those early self-made men, almost a classic case, is James Kershaw (1795–1864), who partnered Callender in the calico-printing firm of Leese, Callender and Co. 'He started life as a warehouse lad, but showed such business qualities that at a tolerably early age he was made a partner . . .' Formerly he had lived in Great Ancoats Street, where his wife carried on a business as a linen draper. He was a member of the Council of the League, an alderman from 1838 to 1850, Mayor 1842–43, and M.P. for Stockport, 1847–59. He was one the the earliest residents of the Park, remaining from 1838 to 1859.

The years after the repeal of the Corn Laws to about 1860 were the golden age of Manchester Liberalism. It was during these years that the largest fortunes were made, politics were still dominated by personalities, and local government was merely a matter for the prominent citizens of the townships.[4] There is no record of any con-

---

[1] *Manchester Weekly Times*, 26th April 1879 (obituary); Whitaker, thesis, p. 37; Axon, *Annals*, p. 372; Prentice, *Anti-Corn-Law League*, Vol. I, p. 69.

[2] Hadfield's daughter survived into the twentieth century, residing in Conyngham Road.

[3] Typical in that he combines all or most of the features found singly or in lesser degree in others of the same era.

[4] Whitaker points out that, as far as the Liberals were concerned, 'The party

tested election for membership of the Rusholme Local Board of
Health—mere nomination was sufficient. Throughout the period,
Park residents appear as leaders in local organizations. Hadfield has
already been mentioned as a leading Congregationalist. The Scots
Presbyterians had, by the 1850s, formed a closely knit little community around All Saints.[1] Robert Barbour, brother of G. F. Barbour,[2] was a leading member of this group. He laid the foundation
stone of their new church in All Saints in 1850. He was closely connected, with E. R. Langworthy, with the re-foundation of the
Grammar School during the 1850s.[3] The Barbour family moved out
of the Park as early as 1860 and settled in Bolesworth Castle in
Cheshire.

Although no research has been done on the growth of the Conservative Party in Manchester during the period, two Park residents
can be cited as Tory equivalents to the Liberal personalities just
mentioned. Both were clearly largely responsible for that revival
which Whitaker hints at, and which must have been as instrumental
in the decline of the Liberal monopoly as the passing of the old
school.

The son of the elder Callender[4] (who has already been mentioned),
William Romaine Callender, jun. (1825–76), was the first of these.
He lived in the Park from 1860 to 1872. Whitaker[5] describes him
as 'the exact antithesis' of his father in religion and politics. In 1874,
he was elected as Conservative member 'in a contest of unparallelled
severity'. 'He had made unsparing sacrifices on its [the party's]
behalf in time, labour and means, his devotion was untiring and
incessant . . . he answered liberally the numerous drafts made on
his purse by the claims of the party . . . there is little doubt that
he gave the chief impetus to whatever of the Conservative reaction
has taken place in South Lancashire.' He advised on municipal
elections and ward organizations, and diligently promoted the district Conservative clubs.

The other great local Conservative of the period was Thomas
Sowler (1818–91).[6] He lived in the Park from 1877 to 1891, and
came from a publishing family, his father promoting and publishing the *Manchester Courier* from 1825 to 1871, when the son took over

---

was only beginning to be concerned with the subject in 1879'. Even as late as the
1880s we find local candidates in Rusholme, 'sinking all political considerations'
(Whitaker, pp. 212–14).

[1] See *Sir Charles Macara* by W. H. Mills, ch. 2, on 'Victorian Manchester'.

[2] *Manchester Guardian*, 20th January 1887 (obituary).

[3] Mumford, ch. 12 and appendix 2, p. 513.

[4] *Manchester Guardian*, 24th May 1872. He lived at 'Ashburne,' where he enter-
tained Disraeli in 1872.

[5] Thesis, p. 26, note; see also Brian Harrison, 'The British prohibitionists, 1853–
1872', *International Review of Social History*, Vol. XV, 1970, p. 433.

[6] *Manchester Courier*, 6th April 1891.

the paper. In 1874 he started the *Evening Mail,* and the *Courier* became a weekly. In both these papers he steadily promoted the Conservative interest. He stood for South Manchester against Roscoe in 1885 and lost by only 300 votes. He was Chairman of the Manchester Conservative Club, and vice chairman of the Political Committee.

The growth of the Park spans the period when the great local and foreign mercantile firms came to dominate the economic life of the city.[1] Table 1 shows this growth. The number of manufacturers remained steady, whilst the number of merchants living inside the

TABLE 1

OCCUPIERS OF HOUSES IN VICTORIA PARK—OCCUPATIONS

	1845	1850	1855	1860	1865	1870	1875	1880	1885
Manufacturer	11	13	12	12	20	17	17	20	21
Merchant	18	25	26	30	47	40	41	41	42
German Merchant*	6	12	15	25	30	40	39	47	39
Professional	4	5	5	6	5	6	15	20	22
TOTAL	39	55	58	73	103	102	112	128	124

* Based on Scholes, 'Manchester Foreign Merchants, 1784–1870' MS, list of foreign firms in the city from 1784 to 1870. After 1870, based on surnames.
Note: This table includes houses put up during the 1870s and 1880s along Clarence Road and what later became Longford Place and which were situated in the Moss Side portion of the Park. See map 3.

region rose steadily. Particularly striking is the growth of the German families living in the Park, which by 1870 numbered as many as one third of the total population. It is also striking that until 1875 the number of professional men remained very small, after which date there was a very considerable increase. The growth of the mercantile class has been traced by Farnie.[2] He writes of the change that took place in the early nineteenth century 'when the manufacturer had

[1] For short, but admirably lucid descriptions of Manchester and the emerging South Lancashire conurbation, see James Bryce's *Report to the Schools Enquiry Commission,* 1864–67, ch. 17, pp. 712 and 749–52. Thus, 'Society has settled down and consolidated itself, manners have grown more refined, and the distinction of classes has become more marked. Thirty years previously the population was composed of operatives and their employers, the millowners, had themselves just risen from the ranks. Now there is a large and tolerably well-defined class of wealthy merchants, commission agents, cotton spinners, and calico printers, and below them a vast body of persons employed by them as warehousemen and clerks at salaries ranging from £60 up to £400, in some few cases, up to £1,000 p.a. Besides the warehousemen, who are in Lancashire at least, quite peculiar to Manchester, there is the usual proportion of professional men, and shopkeepers, great and small.'
[2] D. A. Farnie, 'The English Cotton Industry, 1850–1896', M.A. thesis, Manchester University, 1953.

conducted foreign trade directly'. He relates the growth of this class directly to technological forces; 'with the increase of the amounts of capital locked up in the industry, as machinery was extended and improved, the increased dependence on foreign markets, requiring a highly specialised knowledge, and the progressive diversification of the product made it impossible for the manufacturer of one commodity to have agents in every country'.[1] Of the Germans he writes, 'coming chiefly from Hamburg and Frankfurt on Main, as buying agents for continental customers, they brought with them their alertness, knowledge of foreign languages and entered the South American markets'.

Just as the Liberal Congregationalists and Presbyterians had their own flourishing communities, intermingling in those great general Manchester developments of the University and the grammar schools, so, too, the Germans welded themselves into social life and the mercantile groups. There are literally dozens of names that could be quoted. Leopold Schwabe, for example, who lived in Buckingham Crescent for over 50 years, 'joined Carlos Chaimberlain,[2] Heard and Donner'.[3] Of course, at an early stage young Germans like Emil Liebert, who later became the German consul in Manchester, would find the 'change from German to English life eminently suited to the development of enlightened democratic ideas'. The names of these families appear on the subscription lists from the Anti-Corn-Law League to the movement for the extension of Owens College. The extent to which they were in a very real sense fully integrated into the community may be judged from some quotations from an article by a correspondent in the *Manchester Guardian*, 4th July 1888, on 'Consul Emil Liebert'. The correspondent writes of 'the sons of old Deutschland' and goes on, 'If one proceeded to test the quality of the Manchester Royal Exchange minus its German element, it would almost be like sampling rum punch out of which some malicious mixer had left the rum. Should this seem an exaggeration, let the Master of the Exchange get up and bar the door some day and keep out the Teutons. Echoes of comparative emptiness would ring to the roof!'

The context of the growth of South Manchester is well illustrated by population movement during this period. It is, of course, difficult to get accurate information on buildings and persons. Construction and demolition proceed continually, and can only be traced by very careful study of contemporary maps (when available), ratebooks, or some such record which describes an occupier and an address. Street and house names change, however, and directories are not always reliable.

[1] Farnie, thesis, p. 256.
[2] Carlos Chaimberlain lived at 'Sunbury', 1856–75.
[3] I.e. Edward Donner, see p. 53 (*Manchester Guardian*, 15th June 1888).

That the general pattern of movement outwards must have been taking place, through the Park, is obvious. Probing more deeply, the sort of question one would like to be able to answer would be to enquire into the 'tempo' of immigration into and out of this high-income area. Did the neighbourhoods to the north supply immigrants uniformly, or did many families follow the Hopkinsons along 'tracks' through the suburbs? What percentage came from outside Manchester altogether, and did this overall immigration vary from year to year? Once more, these questions belong more properly to an extended study. However, some material is available and is included here to give a rough idea of what was happening.

An attempt has been made in this study to discover the previous address of every person who lived in the Park between 1840 and 1885. Table 2 shows the result of this enquiry. These addresses fell readily into categories, these categories therefore formed the basis of the analysis. It is to be expected that the three main streets between the Park and Manchester should be supplying new residents. One would expect that the suburbs to the north, through which these streets passed, would also be losing people southward. Of course, except in certain instances, not too much attention should be paid to absolute numbers, since the supplying areas vary in size, these sizes not being known. However, a certain pattern does emerge.

In the first place, if one assumes that those whose addresses cannot be traced came from outside the region, then the years 1845–55 were the highest in this respect. These years were prosperous,[1] and one would expect a higher immigration rate. It was not until 1875 and after that the same rate was again experienced. From about 1855 to 1875, the movement of persons out from the centre into the area was roughly twice the immigration from outside the city. Considering the steady growth of property[2] in the Park, movement in from suburbs to the north remains fairly constant. Thus it is immigration from *outside* the city which varies most. Turning to particular sources, it is interesting to note that the areas considered did not supply immigrants to the Park uniformly, but that in some cases a definite periodicity may be distinguished. Oxford Street was supplying persons regularly up to about 1865, when its place was taken by Rusholme and Moss Side. More striking is the case of Greenheys, which supplied heavily till about 1870, after which date its contribution dropped to about one-third. During the peak immigration period, 1871–75, both Oxford Street and Greenheys supplied only *one* immigrant. Chorlton-on-Medlock, however, after 1870, and particularly after 1875, was rapidly increasing its supply.

It must be admitted that the conclusions are very tentative. In the absence of an overall picture, the data for a part cannot be con-

[1] The railway boom and, after 1849, great prosperity for cotton.
[2] See table 3.

TABLE 2

ANALYSIS OF FORMER ADDRESSES OF PARK RESIDENTS, 1840–1885

	1841–45	1845–50	1851–55	1856–60	1861–65	1866–70	1871–75	1876–80	1881–85	Total
Victoria Park	1	1	5	3	5	6	7	5	3	36
Plymouth Grove	0	3	1	2	1	4	2	3	2	18
Upper Brook Street	1	2	1	3	0	3	2	0	1	13
Oxford Street	3	3	2	4	4	0	0	1	0	17
Chorlton-on-Medlock	1	4	1	5	1	2	4	9	7	32
Greenheys	6	2	4	3	4	6	1	2	1	29
Rusholme	2	1	1	0	1	2	3	0	2	12
Moss Side	0	1	1	0	0	1	3	2	2	10
Ardwick	0	1	2	0	0	1	2	0	1	7
Longsight	0	0	0	0	2	0	2	1	1	6
South of Victoria Park	0	2	0	0	0	1	0	3	2	8
Manchester & North	9	2	2	1	2	0	3	0	1	20
TOTAL	23	22	20	21	20	26	29	26	23	
Not traced	15	23	24	14	13	5	11	24	28	
TOTAL	38	45	44	35	33	31	40	43	51	

clusive. For example, the high rate of movement within the Park, particularly during the years 1866–75, tempts one to infer a desire to stay in the area, especially as these years saw the expansion of suburbs to the south. But unless some idea of the movement from other suburbs out to the south can be obtained, it may be that these higher figures represent merely a generally higher turnover of property.

Thus by analysing previous addresses of Park dwellers, the beginnings of a pattern seem to emerge. The first immigrants came from Greenheys and Oxford Street. Later, after about 1870, Chorlton-on-Medlock supplied an increasing number. But whilst useful as a minor pilot enquiry, it must be admitted that the findings are inconclusive so far, though they seem to fit vaguely the pattern of the expanding city.

This introduction has attempted to sketch the social, economic and political background of Victoria Park. We now turn to the detailed examination of the origin of the scheme, and the promotion of the company.

TABLE 3

VICTORIA PARK, NUMBER OF HOUSES BUILT IN FIVE YEAR
PERIODS*

1837 -45	1846 -50	1851 -55	1856 -60	1861 -65	1866 -70	1871 -75	1876 -80	1881 -85
35	14	15	2	9	3	10	2	8

* Based on Rusholme Rate books, and therefore does not include the five houses in the Moss Side detached part. See map 1.

CHAPTER I

THE VICTORIA PARK COMPANY AND THE VICTORIA PARK TRUST, 1836–1845

In the year 1836 some advertisements appeared in the Manchester press of a projected scheme for the purchase of some 180 acres of land, situated about two miles from the city, mainly in the township of Rusholme. Following on the purchase, an ornamental park was to be formed with plots laid out for mansions and villa residences which were to be sold or let. Eight landowners and merchants[1] agreed to associate for the purchase of the land to form a company and to obtain an act of Parliament to establish the legal status of the company and scheme. A prospectus of the company appeared on 4th April 1836,[2] the Directors were named and the company was floated. The plan of action was, that with the money subscribed by the shareholders, the land of the Park, which lay in Rusholme, Chorlton-on-Medlock and Moss Side,[3] should be bought from the owners, part on lease, should be developed as regards roads and drainage, laid out in plots, and then sold to those who wished to live in the area. This sale would carry with it certain conditions, the 'laws' of the Park, which would protect its amenities. Some of the land was to be sold without houses, the rest in plots fit for building.

The name chosen was in honour of the heir-apparent, the future Queen Victoria. Though the company was not yet a corporate body, application for so many shares had already been made that these were issued in June 1836, various plots were purchased, and Richard Lane[4] was directed to contract for the building of a park wall and entrance lodges. These lodges were begun in August 1836 and the

[1] Thomas Harbottle, merchant   Richard Bentley—merchant
   Joseph Adshead   ,,   Joseph Denison—landowner
   Henry Byrom   ,,   Thomas Bunting—merchant
   John Westhead   ,,   Richard Lane—architect
[2] In the *Manchester Courier*. The prospectus covers well over half a column, and is, like the report of the opening (see p. 15) partly a publicity scheme. The reasons given for the choice of site were 'its contiguity to the best roads leading from that part of the town from which the principal business is rapidly removing, the variety of means of access to it, its total freedom from manufacturers and from their disagreeable effects . . .' (*Manchester Courier*, 4th April 1836.)
[3] See map 1, the Chorlton-on-Medlock portion. Only a few square yards were situated in the extreme north-east. The Moss Side detached portion is clearly visible.
[4] Prominent Manchester architect who worked in classical style, building many local public buildings, e.g. Salford Town Hall (C. Stewart, *Stones of Manchester*.)

land was offered, first to shareholders, and later in September and October 1836[1] to the public, notices of the land offered being sent to various solicitors in the town.

It was in December 1836 that the decision was taken to consolidate the company by an Act of Parliament. The draft was considered shortly after this, and on 5th May 1837, still in the reign of William IV, the Victoria Park Act[2] received the Royal Assent. By this Act, the company received very definite powers, and from it much of the company's early objects and history can be discovered. The Company was formed on the principle of tontine (a form of gambling invented by a Neapolitan banker, Tonti, in 1653) whereby each holder of a £100 share could nominate a 'life'. If the person nominated died within the first three years, then another life could be chosen. As the persons so nominated died off the holders were to lose their shares in the company. When only fifty lives remained, the whole assets were to be divided among the shareholders who had nominated them, in proportion to the shares they each held. This scheme came to nothing, for the company did not survive for a long enough period. The company had the power to lay out and embellish part of its property as an ornamental park with a wall, to lay out streets, squares and crescents, and to erect private dwelling-houses, but not buildings that were applicable for purposes of trade. A penalty was enacted on persons making, selling or using keys for opening the gates of the park without the permission of the directors. Power was granted for raising £500,000 in 5,000 shares of £100 each, for the payment on land and for Park maintenance. The original directors were Thomas Harbottle, Joseph Adshead, Henry Byrom, John Westhead and Richard Bealey. In addition to these, the following are named as originators of the scheme: Joseph Denison, Joseph Ablett, John Dickenson, Frederick William Cobden and Richard Crook. What the Company did was to arrange for the purchase of the land of the Park, even though it did not in the long run actually pay for it all. The total area taken over was 708,667 square yards or approximately 146 acres. The largest sellers were Leicester —236,827 square yards, Adshead—117,231 square yards, Alderson —47,366 square yards. Much of the land in the Park belonged to John Dickenson, owner of the Birch estate. Before the company was formed he sold some of his land to others, who in their turn sold it

[1] See front page of *Manchester Courier*, throughout September and October 1836: 'Victoria Park Tontine ... The Directors are now ready to treat for the sale of plots of land in the Park and also the erection of Houses therein.'

[2] Vol. 92, 1837, of the *Journal of the House of Commons* describes the stages in the passage of the bill, which was presented by Mark Phillips on 3rd March after being petitioned 16th February by 'owners and occupiers of estates and other inhabitants'. Curiously, for reasons which remain obscure, the bill was opposed by a William Froggatt of Manchester. Froggatt lived at Ardwick, but I have been unable to discover any other mention of his activities.

to the Company, and who in some cases bought it back with the restrictions that became attached to the land in the Park.

Richard Lane went ahead with the laying of roads and sewers. The early houses were built around the Oxford Road Crescent entrance and along Oxford Place (see map). By 5th August 1837, the Park was well advanced, for on that day a grand carriage procession made the journey from Manchester and toured the Park. A lengthy report of this procession in *Wheeler's Manchester Chronicle* for that date describes in great detail the attractions of the Park, and the remarks of an impressive array of local notabilities who were present to partake of the 'elegant cold collation' served at the Birch Villa Inn.[1]

After this vigorous launching, it was unfortunate for the promoters of the scheme that the trade depression of 1838–43 plunged the Company into instability. It is impossible to say whether it was only these external economic factors or the complexities of Tontine or even the beginnings of a suspicion that all had not been well in the formation of the Company that caused this. However, bankruptcy threatened in 1838, so the Company appears about that time to have passed out of existence. In later records[2] it is referred to as 'fading away', disposing of its property on the best terms that it could. This meant that, in most cases, it reconveyed to the original owners the land that it still held and had not been able to sell. This reconveyance, with the stipulation from its engagements and arrears of chief rents, appears in the deeds of some of the older houses.

A careful examination of the Rusholme rate books of the period 1838 to 1844 reveals clearly the rate at which houses were built and occupied:

Year	Occupied	Unoccupied	Total*
1838	5	4	9
1839	8	11	19
1840	10	10	20
1841	15	22	37
1842	14	17	31
1843	26	8	34
1844	33	1	34

* The discrepancy in the figure for 'Total' is due to the fact, that 'unoccupied' and 'unfinished' are not used consistently in the rate book. The total figure is merely an addition.

[1] It was reported that '9 elegant mansions (including the residences of Adshead, Lane, Leicester and Hadfield) are already complete or nearly so'. T. Harbottle presided, and among those present were C. Poulett Thomson, M.P., Joseph Brotherton, M.P. and Mark Phillips, M.P.

[2] Notes contained in Bosdin Leech papers, appertaining to the early years of the Company. Also some references in *Foss* v. *Harbottle*. See pp. 16–18.

These figures show a steady rise from 1838 to 1842 in the number of unoccupied properties. The jump in 1841 is due to the fact that the houses situated around the crescent were completed in the previous year. This sharp rise in unoccupied property, despite the fact that the houses along Oxford Place were taken, may have touched off a panic, though it was after the settling of the case of *Foss* v. *Harbottle* that there was a sharp rise in tenancy within the area.

This case[1] provides strong evidence that the disintegration of the original company had not been entirely due to economic causes, or to panic when it was suspected that buildings begun would never be completed or occupied. This Bill alleged (i) that the directors of the Company, including the architect Lane, 'fraudulently concerted and agreed . . . with the object of enabling themselves to derive a personal profit from the said Company; that the plan was that a certain number of them be appointed directors, and should purchase the said plots from the person in whom they were vested, at greatly increased and exorbitant prices, greatly exceeding those at which the said persons had purchased them.

(ii) That some conveyances were taken in the Company's name, others in the name of Directors in trust for the Company, others in agreement only, without conveyance, so that the Company took over the land charged with chief rent due to original owners, also with additional chief rents reserved to seven defendants. That with fraudulent intent, the said directors, after purchasing the said lands for the Company, applied some £27,000 of the Company's money in purchase or redemption of rents reserved to themselves, leaving the land subject to chief rent reserved to the original land owners.

(iii) That the plans and design of the Park were drawn up by Lane, Denison and Bunting, with a view to increasing the value of certain parcels of land belonging to Denison and Lane between the boundary and the Oxford Lodge, that such land was essential to the Company's requirements, according to the plan, that houses there erected would, on being behind the entrance lodge, enjoy the privileges of the Park and that consequently it was sold by Denison and Lane for building land at greatly enhanced prices.'

It appears that at the end of 1839 the Company had discharged its secretary Bramme, had given up its office, and all its books, deeds and papers had been transferred to Bunting. It was therefore contended that the few remaining assets, if left under the control of the present directorate would be dissipated, and no funds would be available to meet the Company's debts, and that the present directors if made responsible could ensure a surplus to pay off these debts.

---

[1] *Foss* v. *Harbottle*. (*English Reports*) Vol. 67, p. 189). Foss was secretary of the Manchester and Birmingham Railway, and lived in Buckingham Crescent from 1842 to 1846. In 1841 Richard Foss was living at 39 Burlington St., Greenheys (information kindly supplied by Mr. J. E. C. Palmer, The British Library).

The defendants contended that the suit complaining of injuries to the corporation was not wholly informed in having only some of its incorporate members before the court; that this defect would not be cured by adding the incorporated company as a party. The defendants claimed the plaintiffs were not entitled to represent the corporate body, even as distinguished from the defendants, and for the purpose of impeaching the transactions complained of.

It was further alleged

that the plaintiffs if they had any ground for impeaching the conduct of the defendants, they might have used the name of the incorporated company, and in that case it would have been open to the defendants as to the body of the directors and proprietors assuming the government of the company, to have applied to the court, for a stay of proceedings, or to prevent the use of the corporate name and upon that application, the court would have enquired into the alleged usurpation or abuse of authority and determined whether the plaintiff should be permitted to proceed.

The judgement turned mainly on the right of individual members of the corporation to take on the responsibilities of the corporation. Thus,

it was not, nor could it be successfully held, that it was a matter of course for any individual member of a corporation, thus to assume to themselves the right of sueing in the name of the corporation. In law, the corporation and the aggregate members of the corporation are not the same thing for purposes like this, and the only question can be, whether the facts alleged in this case justify a departure from this rule which *prima facie* would require that the corporation should sue in its own name and in its corporate character or in the name of someone whom the law has appointed.

Judgement pointed to the fact that there had been in existence a governing body, and it was up to members of the company to deal internally, within the company, with company matters. The existence of such a governing body had been admitted by the plaintiffs:

the Bill, I cannot but observe, is framed with great care, but the averments do not exclude that, which *prima facie*, must be taken to have been the case, that during the years 1840–1842 there was a governing body, the business of the company was carried on, that there was no insurmountable obstacle to the exercise of the powers of the proprietors assembled in the general meeting to control the affairs of the company, and that such meetings were actually held.

It was finally held therefore

that upon the facts stated the continued existence of the board of directors *de facto* must be intended, that the possibility of convening a general meeting of proprietors capable of controlling the acts of the existing board was not excluded by the allegations of the Bill, that is, in such circumstances there was nothing to prevent the company from obtaining redress in its corporate character in respect of the matters complained of and that therefore, the plaintiffs should not sue in a form which assumed the practical dissolution of the corporation and that the demurrers must be allowed.

The case was therefore lost. There is no record that any further attempt was made to recover the lost funds.

In the words of the centenary booklet between 1842 and 1845 the Park 'suffered an interregnum'.[1] The company was either non-existent, or divided amongst itself, and the local township of Rusholme was in no way organized to maintain the property. However, the number of unoccupied houses fell sharply in 1843, though building had for the most part ceased. Already, some persons who were to become prominent in social and political life had taken up residence.[2] By 1845 the residents must have realized that something must be done to clarify their position and the status of the Park. A meeting of landowners and residents was called, at which it was decided to form the Victoria Park Trust. This trust had for its objects the preservation of the area as a private park, and the upkeep of the roads, lodges and the gates. It arranged for an annual election of an executive committee which kept accounts and minute books of all its transactions and proceedings.

Further details about these events is not now available, mainly because the minute books of the company (or trust) from 1845 to 1894 have disappeared,[3] though copies of certain parts, and statements written out for legal purposes[4] when these minute books were able to be consulted still survive. What was important, for the subsequent history of the Park, and particularly in its relations with local government institutions, was the precise status of this committee, and whether it could act legally on behalf of the residents of the Park in dealings with other individuals and corporate bodies. Clearly, there was some argument that it could *not*, since the original Victoria Park Company was still technically in existence, and the new Victoria Park Trust had not the statutory recognition that the Victoria Park Act had bestowed on its ill-fated predecessor. Some half a century later at least one prominent Park resident, himself a lawyer, claimed that the 1845 committee had no legal status or power to act for the residents *in toto*.[5] Nevertheless, the new committee stuck to the letter of the original Act, and kept the Park private. The few surviving account books of the Trust,[6] which date from that period, show the contributions which the inhabitants made to the internal park rate and how these funds were expended on road and lodge upkeep and labourers' wages.

[1] *A Short Account of the Victoria Park*, Manchester, 1937, p. 13.
[2] E.g. Robert Barbour (arrived 1839), James Kershaw, M.P., George Hadfield, prominent Liberal. But see introduction for details, pp. 5-6.
[3] Centenary Booklet, p. 14.
[4] Legal Briefs concerning building tie question. See ch. 5.
[5] R. D. Darbishire in 1902 tramway controversy. See p. 64.
[6] Bosdin Leech papers.

In addition, the few extracts from these very early transactions that survive indicate that it was decided immediately to outline clearly the intended status and powers of the new committee, and the rights and duties of the inhabitants. On 10th March 1845 it was resolved that 'the committee be requested to ascertain whether an Act of Parliament can be obtained for repairing and keeping in order roads . . . and of levying a rate to pay the expenses so incurred'.

There is no evidence of further progress to this end. On 4th April 1845 it was resolved that

it is desirable that the keeping in repair of the roads and the preventing of trespass on the property in Victoria Park should be placed under the management of a general committee of five persons. That a day and night police be authorised to take away any trespassers or persons refusing to leave the park upon being challenged to do so, to prevent the entrance of any carriages or carts improperly seeking to pass through the gates.

The minute claiming the extension of the privacy of the Park draws the distinction between the Park being a thoroughfare and the roads in the Park being used as access to property within the Park. Thus it was resolved, 'that on no account shall the Park be made a public thoroughfare, but that every facility of access be given through the lodges to any house or property within the park'.

The levying of tolls on the roads of the Park dates from this period. Though the tolls were later thought of as a method of maintaining privacy and contributing to the cost of road maintenance, the levy was undertaken on neither of these grounds. In those early days, the road which passes along the extreme western end of the Park, Wilmslow Road, was a turnpike road and subject to toll. A main toll gate before Manchester was situated somewhere between the two sets of park gates, for it was possible to avoid payment of tolls by passing through the Park. The following resolutions taken at the meeting of 11th March 1845 describe the position of the committee:

. . . the committee think it desirable to state that it has been repeatedly under consideration how far it would be desirable to lay a toll on all or a portion of the carriages passing into the Park, or adopt some other means to meet the complaints made by the Trustees of the Turnpike roads of the facilities offered by the Park for the extensive avoidance of the tolls and which the committee now fear prevails.

The resolution actually specifying that tolls were to be levied was passed on 1st April 1846:

The committee recommend that in order to prevent the evasion of the Turnpike road tolls, all vehicles or parties on horseback passing out at different gates from those at which they have entered, shall pay the same rate as is charged by the trustees of the roads. This rule does not apply

C

to residents and their families passing in and out in carriages or on horse-back.

The first chairman of the Park Committee was F. W. Cobden, Richard's brother. Among the papers of the Cobden family, held in the local history library at Manchester, is a short sequence of letters written by Cobden covering the period 1847–52. The secretary of the Committee during this period was Joseph Erhart. Residents of the Park paid contributions to Cobden. One, Leicester, presumably the same man who was originally involved, was being pressed for payment. In 1849 a proposal to open the road at the junction of Clarence Street was sent out by the accountant, Bridgeford, acting on behalf of Joseph Denison, who approached all land-owners in the Park. The proposal was to erect a toll gate and thus shorten the route to Manchester by half a mile and the money would be raised by landowners contributing in proportion to their holding. In 1850 Cobden wrote a letter to the secretary complaining that 'about one third of the tenants have not paid, and very few land-owners will pay the supplementary rate'.

There is no record that these early meetings elected the committees which, in effect, became the governing body of the Park area. As the years passed, the fact that the original company had never been formally wound up added to the tradition that these committees were the direct heirs of the original directors of the company. On the other hand, no trust deeds were ever drawn up, though the committee in its dealings with outside bodies always claimed to be acting on behalf of the whole of the residents. In 1845 the Park was in the position of a private, self-governing rural retreat for merchants and some professional people working in Manchester.[1] It was not until the late 1840s that the adjacent township of Rusholme began to move towards local government. After 1851, when a Local Board of Health was established, and particularly after 1885, when the status of the Park as a private area was once more recognized by Act of Parliament,[2] there were local government institutions which could compete with the Trust Committee in matters of administration within the Park area. The precise extent to which residents of the Park relied on the Trust Committee, in dealing with the Local Board, and vice versa, will be the subject of the following chapter.

[1] According to *Slater's Directory*, there were in 1845 twenty-six merchants living in the Park, six professional men and two whose occupations were unspecified.
[2] See p. 39.

CHAPTER II

VICTORIA PARK AND THE RUSHOLME LOCAL BOARD OF HEALTH, 1848–1885

During the years 1848–85 the township of Rusholme was administered by a Local Board of Health. The Park was for the most part within this township. Hence the residents of the Park had a dual responsibility, and two administrative bodies could (in theory) look after their needs. It is this ambiguity of authority which permits an account of these years to be written despite the loss of the Victoria Park Trust Committee minute books for the years 1845–94.[1] However, the Local Board's Minutes[2] do exist, and by a careful analysis of all references to Victoria Park it is possible to draw some conclusions as to the extent of its powers and activities. This analysis is preceded by a description of the origin of the Board, and the growth of Rusholme and the Park generally.

The Ordnance Survey Map prepared between 1845 and 1848 (map 2) gives a clear indication of the position of Victoria Park in relation to the City of Manchester, whilst map 3[3] shows the position of the Park, in relation to the then unincorporated township of Rusholme. The Park was still well outside the built-up area of the city, there being more or less open country between its northern wall and the Cornbrook stream. To the north-west, the city had started to extend from Greenheys along Lloyd Street and Cecil Street, but the surrounding townships of Moss Side, Chorlton-on-Medlock and Longsight were still quite rural in aspect.[4] Hayes,[5] writing in 1904, speaks of the 1850s thus: 'it was quite a charming walk out to Plymouth Grove, when it was situated in the heart of the country, shaded by its pretty avenues of trees and vocal with the song of birds.' Within the Park itself the effects of the prosperity of the early 1850s[6] added property to the speculative building that had occurred within the Park during the 1840s.[7] Five mansions were erected along the northern side of Oxford Place by the timber

[1] They disappeared some time between 1902 and 1937 when Bosdin Leech failed to find them while gathering material for his centenary booklet.
[2] Rusholme Local Board of Health Minutes (Central Reference Library M/10/23/6).
[3] Prepared for the *Report to the General Board of Health*, 1850.
[4] Blackstake Farm to the north of the Park.
[5] Louis Hayes, *Reminiscences of Manchester from 1840*.
[6] D.A. Farnie. 'The English Cotton Industry, 1850–1896', chap. 26.
[7] Particularly along Buckingham Crescent, 1842, and Addison Terrace, 1848.

merchant, James Bellhouse,[1] whilst E. R. Langworthy,[2] who had built Langdale Hall for himself in 1846–47, built four very large semi-detached houses along Upper Park Road in 1851. All these properties were occupied by merchants.

But the expansion was not confined to the Park. The surrounding township was also growing at what seemed to contemporaries a prodigious pace. The following table shows the expansion of Rusholme during the years 1844–49.[3]

Date	Houses	Population
1844	443	2004
1845	448	2027
1846	457	2068
1847	509	2300
1848	552	2494
1849	627	2834

The township covered 973 acres, which means that Victoria Park made up about a fifth of its total area. The *Report to the General Board of Health* on the township,[4] which gives a detailed picture of conditions in the locality at this time, states:

The village of Rusholme stands on the west side of the township on the road leading to Didsbury. There are about 431 houses and some 2000 inhabitants. Victoria Park (private property) is situated on the north; it consists of about 200 acres of land, which are laid out in gardens, ornamental grounds, roads, etc., for terrace and detached villa residences. There are upwards of 65 houses in this Park at present, and about 390 inhabitants. The population of the township is increasing rapidly. . . . It is now about three times as great as it was 17 years ago. . . . Many new buildings are now in progress.[5]

This report was prepared by Robert Rawlinson, a superintending inspector for the General Board of Health under the Public Health Act of 1848.[6] The Act provides that

in the event of a Petition of not less than one tenth of the inhabitants of the Township[7] a superintending inspector be appointed for the said Act to visit the said Township, and to make a public enquiry, and to examine witnesses as to the drainage and supply of water, the state of the burial

---

[1] The Bellhouse family, though a well-known Manchester family, do not seem to have been prominent in political affairs.
[2] E. R. Langworthy (1797–1874), Mayor of Salford 1848–55; partner in firm of Langworthy Bros. Public benefactor, giving liberally to the Grammar School (Mumford, p. 342–5) and Owens College (Thompson, p. 640).
[3] *Report to the General Board of Health*, 1850, Robert Rawlinson.
[4] *Ibid.*, pp. 10–11.   [5] *Ibid.*, p. 10.   [6] *Ibid.*, para. 6.
[7] *Ibid.*, para. 8. The number of petitioners exceeded 30, though they are not named (*Report*, p. 4).

grounds, the number and sanitary condition of the inhabitants, and as to any local acts of Parliament in force within such Township, for paving, lighting, cleansing, watching, regulating, supplying with water, or improving the said Township, or having relation to the purposes of the said Act.

Rawlinson painted a pretty appalling picture of conditions within his area of inspection. In particular, he complained of the lack of public lighting: '. . . there are no public lights in the Township. The Manchester Corporation have laid their mains out so far, but the gas has not been used, because there is no public governing body to treat for it.'[1] There were no police patrols of a public nature: 'there is a county police, but the number does not allow of more than one man for two such townships. There are four private watchmen.'[2] Rawlinson also complained of the general lack of road maintenance, most of the roads 'being private property, are for the most part, unformed, undrained, and unpaved. The streets are set out by the land owners to suit private convenience. . . . There is no general comprehensive scheme, whereby the convenience and advantage of the whole district is considered.'

In writing of his personal inspection, Rawlinson makes no mention of the Victoria Park Act; indeed he specifically states, 'there is no act in force for self-government and local regulation', though a few lines later he writes, 'There are no public walks or recreation grounds other than Victoria Park, which is private property, and which is dealt with as such.'[3] Of course, Rawlinson was principally concerned with overcrowding, and insanitary conditions, and so it is unlikely that he would have had much to say about the Park. His remarks seem to indicate that towards the end of the 1840s the Trust Committee was operating in respect of road maintenance. The Ordnance Survey Map (map 2) shows an extensive and regular tree plantation, though there is nothing on the map to show that the roads were maintained in any better condition than those in the rest of the township. It is therefore likely that contemporaries conceived of the private roads of the Park as similar to turnpike roads, still operating extensively in the neighbourhood. The Park would be merely a privately maintained area, of an unusually large kind, and in no sense an anomaly.

There is no evidence that the Park Committee, then still in its infancy, made any public attempt to influence the inquiry.[4] Of the twelve principal witnesses present, only two[5] were dwelling within

[1] *Ibid.*, p. 16.
[2] *Ibid.*, p. 17. *Slater's Directory* for 1851 shows Victoria Park as employing two keepers and one constable.
[3] *Ibid.*, p. 17.
[4] The inquiry was held on 3rd August 1849. The report is dated August 1850.
[5] James Ewart, Albert Lodge 1842–54 (land surveyor): John Railton, Park Crescent 1840–58 (agent).

the confines of the Park, though a Mr. Ewart[1] seems to have played a prominent part in the proceedings, and may well have been a leading member of the Trust Committee or its secretary. In general terms, Rawlinson recommended the introduction of a comprehensive system of lighting, drainage and sewage disposal to be supervised by a Local Board of Health as provided under the 1848 Act. This recommendation was granted.

The 1848 Public Health Act provided for the election[2] of a Local Board of Health for the township. The Board had powers over those sanitary matters already mentioned, in particular having powers of purchase, inspection and appointment of officers to inspect sanitary arrangements. Notification of building and registration of lodging houses and abattoirs were also required. Certain powers of construction (e.g. public baths) were also admitted.

The minute books of this Board from its inception in 1851, until its functions were taken over by Manchester in 1885, are available.[3] These books show all proceedings of the Board, all officials, members, all expenses incurred and all recommendations and directives issued in respect of public health matters within the township. As far as this period of the Park's history is concerned, these books comprise the only continuous unified body of material that is available, particularly in reference to local government. In addition, a further enquiry was made in 1855 as to the desirability of including the detached portions of Moss Side within the township of Rusholme.[4] The report of this enquiry[5] also provides evidence of the state of the Park and powers of the Committee at this time. First, however, the material provided by the Local Board Minutes will be considered, leaving the second enquiry till later.

Of the thirty-two references in the Local Board's Minutes to Victoria Park residents, eleven do not concern 'pressure' as defined, and are for the most part in the form of 'resolutions'. Four of these are concerned with matters *outside* the Park, in which some Park dwellers were concerned. One involves the appointment of a sub-committee, to confer with the Victoria Park Trust Committee on the question of general lighting within the Park.[6] Four involved general resolutions about the area. The other two are concerned with particular matters within the area. From the remaining twenty-

---

[1] He 'proved the due advertising and affixed notices as the Act directs'. (p. 4).
[2] The Act provided for the election of twelve members who had to be residents and ratepayers of the Township, on a property qualification of £50 per vote up to six votes, on rateable value. One third of the members were to retire annually.
[3] Manchester Central Reference Library, M/10/26/6.
[4] Map 1.
[5] *Report to the General Board of Health on a Further Enquiry at Rusholme*, by A. L. Dickens, 1855.
[6] 'Mr King and Mr. Bridge were appointed a deputation to meet the Victoria Park Committee in reference to the placing of lamps in that Park' (Minutes 3rd January 1866). Neither of these gentlemen were Park residents.

one references it is clear from this distribution that the Trust Com-mittee was in no way acting as a major factor in local government affairs at this time. There are ten examples of the individual Park dwellers attempting to influence the Local Board of Health on their own behalf, and six examples of the Board contacting individual Park residents. Both these classes involve the by-pass of the Trust Committee as a *possible* channel of administration. Of the remaining five references, four are from the Trust Committee to the Local Board, about the Park as a whole, whilst the other is of the same nature, but in the reverse direction. There were no examples of the Board attempting to influence individuals on Park matters or the Park Committee on individual matters. Neither was there any ex-ample of the Park Committee having dealings with the Local Board of Health about the affairs of any individual resident or his residence in the area.

Several aspects of the Board's activities affected the Victoria Park region. Early in 1852 we find the Local Board making enquiries concerning the need for and the cost of public lighting throughout its district. On 13th December 1852 the following resolution was passed: 'Each street in the district shall be lighted so soon as the same shall be sewered. Also that certain other streets as the Board may from time to time think necessary.' Two years later a motion 'that the whole district be lighted' was put, but was not seconded.

The first mention of the residents of Victoria Park occurs on 7th November 1855 when 'a memorial was received from all the in-habitants and rate payers residing in that part of the Township which is in Victoria Park, asking the Board to light the roads in that Park with gas . . .' The Board discussed this memorial but 'further consideration was deferred'. Very little could have been done, however, about the lighting of the region, for some three years later (4th November 1857) once more a memorial was received from a *section* of the Park,

A memorial was received from 26 owners of property in Victoria Park asking for Daisy Bank Road to be lighted was read, and referred to Mr. Pershouse and Mr. Atkinson to confer with the clerk on the evidence regarding the circumstances of the road, and if necessary, to take the opinion of counsel hereon, so far as the Board may be justified in lighting the same.

There is no evidence that anything was done immediately about this question.[1] However, on 7th November 1860 a resolution was passed which was certainly the first example of the Trust Com-mittee coming into the conflict with the local authority over right of way. The Board had authority to light those thoroughfares along which the public passed freely. The following resolutions indicate

[1] See p. 27. The second enquiry throws some light on the position in 1855.

that the Park Committee were obliged to distinguish between 'public roads' and 'footpaths' in the notices which they placed at the entrances to the Park. The first resolution reads 'that the committee of the Victoria Park be requested to alter their notice placed at the entrance to such Park by inserting in such notice after the words "there is no public road through 'this Park' ", the words, "except on footpaths", with a view to this Board considering lighting the footpaths in the Park'. It is impossible to decide the extent of any disagreement between the Park Committee and the Board. The resolution was passed unanimously, and two of the members present were Park residents. It therefore seems more likely that this change was made to enable the Park to be lighted at the expense of the Local Board. Some months later it was resolved 'that the alteration in the notice at the entrance to the Victoria Park having taken place by the Victoria Park Committee, eleven lamps, in addition to the seven belonging to private persons, they giving them to the Board, be placed in Daisy Bank Road, Victoria Park, . . . at the expense of this Board'. It was also resolved at the same meeting that 'five lamp pillars be erected along Anson Road and lighted'. Of the five members present at this meeting, only one dwelt within the Park boundaries (5th December 1860).

After this date there was a steady stream of requests from individuals and groups of residents for lighting improvement along particular streets within the Park. There is some evidence that some effort was made to treat the Park as a unit in a reference to a plan in a resolution proposed by Pershouse and seconded by O. A. Ferris, the only two residents present at the meeting of eight.

An example of request on behalf of small groups is given by the following. 'A letter was read from Mr. Edward Thomson[1] on behalf of residents in Upper Park Road, applying to have two or three extra lamps put up in that road. It was moved that the subject be referred to the Surveying Committee' (5th November 1862). In 1863 a memorial signed by 17 ratepayers asking for additional lamps was received, the signatories stating 'that their claim to these additional lamps is strengthened by the fact that 13 new houses of a valuable class have been built since lamps were first placed in this Park'.

There are but two examples of individuals writing to the Local Board. John Leisler, of Stoneywood, Lower Park Road, one of the original inhabitants, complained, 'the street lamp before my house in Victoria Park being the only one which at present is not lighted, and out of order, not being taken like all the others under the Town, or Township's management, I request you urgently to put it before the Board. To get this street lamp under the same management, any

---

[1] Merchant, resided at West View, Upper Park Road, 1859/66.

expense I shall be willing to pay . . .' It was resolved that the request made, subject to the offer, be complied with.[1]

There are several other examples[2] of groups of residents, on much the same lines as those already mentioned. The following conclusions may therefore be drawn concerning local government administration at this time.

   (i) The Local Board of Health was prepared to assume responsibility for lighting in Victoria Park by placing lamps and taking over those that had been privately owned.

  (ii) The work was effected mainly as a result of pressure from individuals or small groups interested in very small localities.

 (iii) Though it is clear that the Park was thought to be a special area, there is only little evidence of wholesale treatment by the Board of Health and no evidence of direct pressure by the Park Committee.

It will be convenient to describe at this stage in the narrative the second enquiry, held in 1855, which was concerned with the detached portion of Moss Side, lying almost wholly within the Park boundaries. Once more, there is evidence of the existence of the Park Committee, but it is even more clear from this report that the interests of the Park and of the area in general were seen as identical by those concerned at the time.

In March and August 1855 the Local Board petitioned the General Board 'with reference to an alteration and extension of the boundaries of the district, so as to include certain sections of Moss Side'.[3] The grounds for these inclusions, as stated by Callender, were that the districts referred to were small but inconvenient to handle administratively, and practical islands in the Township of Rusholme. One of these portions lay in the north-west of the Park, occupying about one sixth of the area, and containing some dozen or so properties within the Park, and some fronting Dickenson Road. Of course, the chief bone of contention can be diagnosed as rates or prospective demand for rates. If the Township of Moss Side was to be given a Local Board of its own it would not wish to lose potential value. Consequently there was strong objection from 'a meeting of ratepayers convened by the overseers of the Township of Moss Side'. Naturally, the Rusholme Board could increase their income by incorporating the areas, whilst the inhabitants of those portions in Victoria Park claimed that since they were already paying a rate to the Park Committee, 'a manifest injustice would be done to the

---

[1] Local Board Minutes, 1870.

[2] E.g. from residents of Addison Terrace in February 1878.

[3] *Petition to the General Board of Health on a further enquiry at Rusholme* by A. L. Dickens, 1855. The enquiry was precipitated by an enquiry into the sanitary condition of Moss Side and the expected creation of a Moss Side Local Board of Health. See map 1 for the parts of Moss Side which lay in Victoria Park.

inhabitants generally by subjecting them to double rates and expenses.'

The reluctance of these Park dwellers to be included inside Rusholme with the rest of the residents may be judged from the fact that there was 'a special meeting of the ratepayers of that part of Moss Side situated in Victoria Park and Longsight'. At this meeting a representation was tabled to the General Board of Health's inspector. The Park Committee acted against the wishes of these persons. This representation stated,

that the chief portion of this detached part of Moss Side forms part of Victoria Park, and is under the immediate inspection of surveyors and inspectors appointed by the Park Committee who levy rates upon the inhabitants for the purpose of effecting such improvements as are found to be necessary; that the Park Committee have long since formed excellent roads and have drained and sewered the whole of the Park, and that therefore the necessity of putting the Public Health Act into force in this part of Moss Side does not exist.[1]

The residents of this portion of Moss Side therefore acted as a group, whether they were inside Victoria Park or not. The resolution was proposed by Richard Holt, who lived at Birch House, Longsight, and was seconded by Joseph Broadie of Birch Hall Lane. Neither of these properties were inside Victoria Park. However, the meeting was chaired by John Atkinson, who lived at Daisy Bank House.

Some weight is added to the view that the leading Park dwellers[2] made good use of the Local Board machinery to light the Park, or rather that part of the Park which lay in Rusholme. Dickens, in recommending the annexation of the detached portion, described Oxford Road–Daisy Bank Road thus:

there is an excellent road from Rusholme, which passes through this part of Moss Side to the Manchester and Stockport turnpike road. It is lighted with gas in Rusholme, as also is the turnpike road, but the intermediate portion of Moss Side, a distance of a few hundred yards, is not lighted at all. Thus the inhabitants have a good and well lighted road to either end of the district, while they, to save themselves expense, keep their portion of the thoroughfare in darkness and indifferent repair.[3]

Dickens recommended 'that the detached portion of Moss Side (Part of Victoria Park) situated at the north-east corner of Rusholme, by which township it is bounded on three sides, should be included in the Rusholme district'.[4]

Under the Public Health Act, 1848, and the Local Government Act, 1858, the Local Board of Health was given power for the maintenance and repair of public highways. During the whole of this

---

[1] *Report*, p. 16.
[2] W. R. Callender must have been a prominent member of the Trust Committee. He was chairman of the Local Board, 1852–55.
[3] *Inquiry*, p. 17.   [4] *Ibid.*, p. 17.

period 1851–85 there are only two references to the roads within the Park area. Both indicate clearly that there was never any question of the Local Board taking over the responsibility for maintaining the roads of the Park. The first example, mentioned in October 1859, refers to a letter, read from Mr. Lazerus 'about the repair of Anson Road and the putting up of a lamp there'. It was decided that 'the road was a private one, and the Board would repair it at the owners' expense if they wished it'. Once more, in 1871, 'the surveyor was directed that this Board are not liable for the repair of any part of the Rusholme entrance to Victoria Park, except the width of the footpath'.

An issue which directly involved a number of Park residents, and which foreshadowed the struggles that were to take place later between the Park and Manchester Corporation, was raised by the need for the efficient maintenance of the main roads out of the city to the south, two of which passed the entrances to the Park. Till about the middle of the century the surface had been ordinary macadam, but with the growth of traffic into the expanding township of Rusholme, the expense involved in maintaining such a surface began to warrant the consideration of applying a more durable and slightly more costly surface, which would result in a long-term saving. Of course, better road surfaces go along with increased traffic, the one at once necessitating and then causing the other.

In October 1866 the Law Clerk reported the matter as follows:

I have to report to the Board that I think that their attention should be given to the state of Didsbury road, and the great expense the repair of it imposes on the rate payers in consequence of it being macadamised . . . the roads should be gradually paved with sets commonly called Welsh granite, or other such sets, and that thereby in due course, a great saving would be effected.

After receiving permission to borrow to cover the cost, and after comparing the cost of both surfaces, it was resolved that 'in the opinion of this Board, it is desirable that the Wilmslow Road for its full length through the district be paved with Welsh granite sets . . .'[1] The Board divided on this issue, but the motion was carried by five votes to three. Two of those voting against were Park residents. Opposition to this threat to land values must have been substantial, for the Board was obliged to hold an enquiry into the state of opinion in the township. A circular was duly printed and 853 copies were distributed.[2] One hundred and seventy-six replies in favour of paving and 316 replies in favour of macadamizing were received, whilst twenty-eight were returned 'for the reason that the person to whom they had been addressed could not be found'. At

[1] Minutes, 7th November 1866.   [2] Minutes, 3rd March 1869.

the same meeting a memorial was read signed by twenty-nine residents of the townships, of whom seven were resident in Victoria Park, and a further four had been at some previous time resident. At the time three out of nine of the Local Board were Park residents, but the name of only one of these appears in the minute book as a signatory of the petition. There is no mention of the Park, and no evidence that these Park dwellers who did sign were acting other than as ratepayers within the township.

In this case therefore we may conclude that, although the reasons adduced for the petition both in particular and generally would apply to the region of Victoria Park, particularly those relating to traffic and land values, no concerted action was taken by the Park Committee. This is in marked contrast to the later efforts of the Park to prevent the intrusion of the expanding city.

Briefly, the petition stated that 'the memorialists have come to reside in the district from its social character devoid of nuisance and having agreeable roads to traverse' and that though the expense may be lessened, 'yet your memorialists would prefer a small additional rate to having an injury done to an agreeable residential district'. 'That the proposed course will materially injure the tradesmen on the road, as it will prevent many who keep carriages from coming to the town and who will thus transfer their business to the city.' And finally, 'that the district being thus spoiled, land will be less sought for, and property will be depreciated and the whole character of the district changed, and a lower class of property erected. . . .'

The majority of the ratepayers must have wanted the proposed alterations, for successive sections of the road were paved till by 1874 the whole, as far as Fallowfield, was completed.[1]

In addition to lighting and road maintenance, the two other principal matters which concerned the Local Board of Health were sewers and the removal of nuisances. The latter, the Board had power to abate or remove, but there is evidence that they acted in a contradictory manner. For example on 3rd June 1861 'a letter from Mr. Williams was read in reference to a nuisance in Kent Road and one in a pond, when the law clerk was directed to reply to it that the Board could not interfere on account of the matter being done in Victoria Park'. On the other hand, with the lapse of time it seems that either the Park had lost some of its local autonomy or the Board was better aware of its jurisdiction, for in the minute for 2nd October 1867 'a letter from residents in Anson Road was read in reference to a nuisance in a field behind Mr. Ingham's house. . . .' The nuisance was subsequently removed. In the first instance at the relevant meeting only one out of four present was a resident in Vic-

---

[1] Minutes, 4th March, 1870.

toria Park, in the latter example, four out of six of those present were residents, including Mr. Ingham himself. Although there are several other references to nuisances in the area, in all cases the question was referred to the surveying committee and was presumably dealt with privately.

On one occasion, the Park did act in unison and very probably through the Trust Committee, though there is no mention of that body. It is stated that Mr. Callendar (senior),[1] Mr. Slagg,[2] Mr. Todd, and Mr. Bannatyne, attended with a memorial of which the following is a copy:

We, the undersigned, owners and occupiers of houses in Victoria Park and neighbourhood, have heard with regret that it is proposed to remove the present cabstand from its present position, to the road which forms the entrance to Victoria Park. Such a course would, in our opinion, inflict a serious injustice on the undersigned, a great nuisance would be caused thereby, as well as considerable injury to property. We beg therefore to protest against this change, and request that the Board will reconsider their decision in this matter.

The petition was signed by thirty people. Twenty-nine of these were Park residents, the thirtieth, one Julius Ergoman, cannot be traced. The four persons who attended were very probably members of the Park Committee. At the next meeting it was resolved 'that half the present cab-stand near Moss Grove be removed 100 yards to the south and that the other half be removed to the westerly side of the road opposite the southerly entrance to Victoria Park'. In the matter of drainage, the Park had been sewered by Lane, the original architect. Under the 1848 Act the Board became owners of existing public sewers, had the power to purchase sewers and to inspect and direct their proper maintenance. There is no example of the Board having dealings with the Park as a whole in this matter. Presumably, for the most part, existing sewers, some of which remained till quite recently, were adequate. The Board placed sewers in the Park as early as 1854, and there are some examples of the Board directing ratepayers to attend to their sewers. There is nothing to suggest that they received treatment different from any other ratepayers in the township.

This chapter has been concerned with the Park and local government administration. It has been its intention to show, obliquely, some of the activities of the Trust Committee during this formative period of urban Local Government. In general, the conclusion is that the administrative functions of the Local Board did not greatly affect the interests of the inhabitants of Victoria Park. There were seldom any plain issues of Victoria Park *versus* Rusholme, and for the most part it was true that when prominent citizens dwelt there,

[1] See Introduction, p. 5.   [2] See chap. V, p. 51.

they were likely to be prominent in both Local Board and Park Committee. Those matters which came within the jurisdiction of the Board were dealt with by its officials and the individuals concerned, despite the fact that Rawlinson's original report to the General Board of Health had referred to the area as 'private property'. The Board left the privacy of the Park entirely intact, except for the minor change that foot traffic could not now be prevented, since part of the roads inside the Park were 'footpaths' and were lighted by the Board as such.

CHAPTER III

THE EFFECT ON VICTORIA PARK OF THE INCORPORATION OF RUSHOLME IN THE CITY OF MANCHESTER, 1885

It is beyond the scope of this book to analyse and describe in detail the complex social forces which made up the great changes which took place in the city during the last quarter of the nineteenth century. The superficial facts are obvious and comparatively easy to discover. While the social composition of the Park was just beginning to change and the very first institutions were entering it, both the spread and increase of population generally was making the old administrative boundaries unrealistic. Manchester township experienced a decrease of population during the decade 1871–81, which continued during the following decade. The inner township of Hulme experienced a similar decrease. Chorlton-on-Medlock lost over 2,000 persons from 1891 to 1901. The pattern which emerges is, if conceived graphically, a series of peaks reached by the townships in and surrounding the city, as the concentration of the city population passed through them. By the 1880s the expansion of the built-up area of South Manchester had reached a line roughly parallel with the northern boundary of the Park. To the west, Moss Lane East was the southern edge of the built-up area, and immediately south of this line, except for the band of country which fronted the Wilmslow Road, open fields stretched into Cheshire. Immediately to the north, land fronting Upper Brook Street had been occupied by terraced houses during the 1870s and away to the north-east Longsight was now completely built up.

It must have been clear by the mid-1880s that administrative reorganization would have to follow these physical changes. From the point of view of the city of Manchester, there were several reasons why the townships adjacent should be incorporated within its boundaries. Some ten years earlier, the townships within the city boundary had been regrouped together for rating purposes. The success of this measure paved the way for extension. Secondly, Manchester controlled property outside the city boundaries. Thirdly, 'many Manchester wage earners lived outside the city boundaries and it was likely that as tramway services were extended, a greater exodus would take place'[1]. In addition,

[1] Redford, Vol. ii, p. 213.

the out-townships were . . . dependent on the rate payers of Manchester for the supply of gas, water, markets, public parks, cemeteries, free libraries, baths and washhouses, and schools. Some of these advantages were obtained without any payment, and although in other instances there might be a differential rate as against outsiders, this circumstance by no means counterveiled the immense benefit which the suburbs derived from the city. It would be well that the whole district known as 'Manchester' should be comprised within the city boundary.[1]

Finally, the extension of the physical area of the city had been accompanied by only piecemeal provision by the city for its supply of gas and water, thus,

it may be roughly estimated that a radius of four miles from the Town Hall would comprise a population of exceeding three quarters of a million, under the jurisdiction of not less than twenty-two sanitary authorities (for the most part urban) all of which, with one exception, receive the Manchester Town's water and sixteen of which are supplied with Manchester gas. Any minor scheme should be abandoned, the extension of the boundaries shall be far-reaching and comprehensive.[2]

The general advantages accruing to individual townships if able to become incorporated with the city may be illustrated by the example of Newton Heath, a township lying to the north-west. At the Local Board of Health's meeting, 11th February 1880, most of these were expressed in a resolution,[3] 'difficulties have arisen in respect to roads, in which both authorities are more or less concerned . . .' The burdens of a small authority within a comprehensive scheme recur: '. . . the City Council have propounded a sewage scheme . . . which your memorialists feel to be a great necessity for the district, but, as a separate authority, could not bear the expense estimated for it'. The growing economic and social unity of the township with the city is well illustrated here, '. . . the demolition of so many dwelling-houses in the city has driven hundreds of families into the suburbs to reside, whilst their occupations or places of work remain in the city'.[4]

On 6th December 1882, it was resolved that 'communications be forwarded to the authorities of Bradford, Newton Heath and Harpurhey, to arrange interviews on the subject of incorporation'. On 6th December 1882 representatives from the three townships attended, 'stating in general terms their desire to be in the city'.[5] The Council declared its desire for a greater 'extension of the city boundaries than would be involved by the admission of the districts represented . . .' The questions of the conditions which 'the corporation

[1] H. Rawson, *An Historical Record of some recent Enterprises of the City of Manchester*, 1894.
[2] See Redford, Vol. ii, pp. 314–15.
[3] *Manchester City Council Proceedings*, 1879–80, p. 225.
[4] *Council Proceedings*, 1879–80, pp. 226–7.
[5] *Council Proceedings*, 1882–83, p. 76.

would require as to paving, sewering and highways . . . and the effect of incorporation on the permanent officials of the incorporated districts' were particularly discussed.

The negotiations continued throughout 1883. The Corporation was eager to incorporate, as indeed were the townships, the latter insisting 'that it should be made a condition that, until their streets and sewers are put into a satisfactory state, equal to the standard of the city, separate rates for the purpose of paving, sewering and highways should be levied and expended in each of these townships'.[1] 1885 saw the incorporation of Bradford, Harpurhey and Rusholme. Newton Heath waited five years because of disagreements over rating and representation.[2]

On 6th July 1881, the Rusholme Local Board of Health received a letter from the Town Clerk of Manchester, requesting the views of the Board as to the desirability of incorporating the district within the city of Manchester.[3] A sub-committee consisting of Messrs. Ramsay, Wren, Ingham, Royle and Bridge was appointed to consider the subject. Apparently Rusholme was by no means as eager for incorporation as the other townships mentioned, for while there is no mention of incorporation in the *Council Proceedings*,[4] or the Local Board of Health Minutes, on 4th July 1883 in the latter it appeared that 'the Law Clerk received an invitation from the Town Clerk of Manchester for the committee appointed on 6th June 1881 to confer with the Corporation'.

Both the City and the Local records report the bare fact that incorporation seemed to offer no advantage at this time: 'The deputation appointed by the Board to confer with the Manchester Corporation as to Incorporation recorded the result of their interview. It was moved by Mr. Heywood and seconded by Mr. Wren, that the Board are not at present satisfied that any advantage would result to the inhabitants of Rusholme from Incorporation with Manchester.'[5]

It may have been the ostensible successful negotiations of the other townships that further prompted Rusholme, but in the minute for 3rd December 1884 there are the elaborate proposals by the Rusholme Board, including the proviso about the Park, which was finally written into the Act. In the matter of the incorporation of Rusholme, there is definite evidence that the Victoria Park Trust Committee interfered in local politics in the interests of the Park residents. Victoria Park lies to the north of the townships, occupying a substantial part of its total area. Hitherto, it had seemed that

[1] *Council Proceedings*, 1883–84, p. 205.
[2] Redford, Vol. ii, p. 317.
[3] Rusholme Local Board of Health Minutes.
[4] This is probably why Redford's account of Rusholme's incorporation is singularly thin.
[5] Local Board of Health Minutes, 4th July 1883.

there had been an identity of interests between the Park Committee and the Local Board. On incorporation matters would be different, Victoria Park would cease to be a large part of the surrounding administrative region, its importance within the local government framework must dwindle, so it was up to the inhabitants of the Park to use the machinery of the Trust Committee, and the constitution of the Local Board, to protect the interests of the Park against mighty Manchester. Park dwellers had no majority on the Local Board of Health either in 1883 or 1884.[1] But later pressure was strong for incorporation, mainly because of sewerage difficulties. Thus, in the report of the Local Board's meeting, Mr. Ramsay (chairman), of Birch Polygon, Rusholme, said in reply to a suggestion of a twelve-month delay: 'It is not a question of waiting twelve months, but a question of dealing with sewage . . . the council should be told of the importance to them of their going on with the Bill.'[2] In this Rusholme had the support of Withington, whose streams were taking much of Rusholme's sewage. Mr. Fuller, the chairman of that Local Board, said on 16th May 1885, 'the sewage within the district of Rusholme, which flowed into the streams and sewers flowing through the district of Withington, should be diverted forthwith'.[3]

The terms of the proposals to the City Council from the Board, as set out in 3rd December 1884[4] deserve to be quoted in full, because of the light they throw on the care with which the owners of property (and hence the residents of Victoria Park) were able to decide the issue, and hence protect the Park residents:

It was moved by Mr. Heywood and seconded by Mr. Jewsbury and unanimously resolved that the Board is desirous of making an arrangement with the Manchester Corporation for the inclusion of the Rusholme district of the city of Manchester on the following terms:

(a) That an agreement between the Corporation of Manchester of the one part and the Rusholme Local Board of the other part embodying paragraphs 3, 4, 5 and 6 of this resolution be entered into

(b) that immediately hereafter the Rusholme Board shall call a meeting of the occupiers and ratepayers of Rusholme for the purpose of obtaining their sanction to such agreement,

(c) in the event of such sanction being obtained, the Rusholme Board shall co-operate with the Corporation of Manchester in obtaining an Act of Parliament to include the district of Rusholme within the boundaries of the city.

(d) The Parliamentary expenses incurred by the Corporation or the Board shall be paid by the Corporation of Manchester,

---

[1] 1883. Ramsay, Royle, Jones, Estcourt, *Jewsbury*, Davies, *Wren*, Payne, Bridgen, Heyland.
1884. Ramsay, Royle, Jones, Estcourt, Payne, *Jewsbury*, Heywood.
[2] *South Manchester Gazette*, 9th May, 1885.
[3] *South Manchester Gazette*, 16th May 1885.
[4] Local Board of Health Minutes.

(e) the said Bill shall contain clauses to the following effect,

(i) Victoria Park shall remain and be a private Park as at present, the public shall be entitled to no right of way therein except on foot, nevertheless the occupiers shall be rated to the city rate, and the occupiers of houses shall be supplied with gas and water at the same rate as the occupiers of houses in the City of Manchester.

(ii) The Corporation of Manchester shall execute such works as may be necessary to direct the sewage of Rusholme ... taking the said sewage into the sewers of Manchester ... the cost to be paid out of the city rate.

(iii) The Corporation of Manchester shall not require the owners of property already existing at their own expense to convert their privies and ashpits to accord with the system adopted by the Corporation ...

(iv) The rate to be levied in the district of Rusholme shall be the same as that of the City of Manchester.

(v) The representation of Rusholme in the City Council shall be arranged by the Corporation and the City of Manchester.

(vi) The clause in the present bill granting compensation to officers shall be extended to Rusholme.

(f) In case the agreement shall not be sanctioned by the property owners and rate-payers of Rusholme, it shall be null and void, and the Corporation shall not seek to incorporate Rusholme in the said City.

At this point it is appropriate to quote a letter, contained in the Bosdin Leech papers, which was written by H. T. Crofton,[1] who must have been a prominent member of the Trust Committee at the time of the incorporation agreement. The letter was written in 1902 to the *then* secretary of the Trust, who must have been seeking advice on how to deal with the Corporation over the matter of the proposed tramways extension.[2] The letter shows quite clearly that the Park residents could control (if acting together) the rest of the residents of the district, as they were by far the largest group of property owners and rate payers. Crofton wrote:

In 1885, under the Public Health Act of 1875[3] the multiple voting put the destinies of Rusholme altogether in the hands of the Park, and to gain the desired end, the Corporation conciliated the Park by Section 48 of the Extension Act.

It was the outcome of interviews with the Local Board.[4] The owners feared that incorporation would mean that they would be called upon to resewer the roads, and both owners and occupiers feared the introduction of paving stones which would destroy the privilege and repose of the residents and lessen values terribly. We asked for a clause expressly vetoing paving,

[1] H. T. Crofton, solicitor and prominent local historian, who wrote histories of local townships, e.g. Stretford and Moss Side.

[2] See chap. VI.

[3] 38 and 39 Victoria. cap. 55. Gave votes to owners and occupiers as follows: £10–50 = 1 vote, £51–100 = 2 votes, £101–150 = 3 votes, £151–200 = 4 votes, £201–250 = 5 votes, £251 and over — 6 votes on rateable value.

[4] These 'interviews' are mentioned neither in Council Proceedings nor in the minutes of the Local Board.

but the Corporation said that Victoria Park would not last forever and it was not right to tie their hands forever, but they assured us that it would not suit their interest to alter the character of the place, and we have no fear of having paving being forced on us.

The precise order in which steps were taken to guarantee the privacy of the Park reveals the way in which the Park Committee engineered their victory. On 4th March 1885 the clause in the draft agreements concerning Victoria Park was amended thus: 'Moved by Mr. Jewsbury and seconded by Mr. Wren[1] and resolved that the printed memorandum of terms of Incorporation with Manchester be approved of, subject to the addition of the following words to clause 5 sub-section (a), "and have all the privileges of the rate-payers of Rusholme living outside the Park." ' It remained only to get the incorporation agreement containing the Victoria Park safeguard clause accepted by the people of Rusholme.

On 18th March 1885 two meetings were held, both with Mr. Ramsay in the chair. They appear on successive pages of the minute books. At the first, 'It was moved by the chairman, and seconded by Mr. Wren, that in the judgment of this Board it is expedient to carry out the arrangement between the Board and corporation, for the inclusion of Rusholme within the proposed extended city of Manchester . . .' The minute for the following meeting reads as follows: 'The notice convening the meeting in pursuance of a requisition of owners and ratepayers was read. Such a meeting was called for the purpose of considering and (if they thought fit) passing the following resolution,' (i.e. the motion as at previous meeting). The resolution was *not* put to the meeting, which was adjourned for a week.

At the adjourned meeting, curiously enough, 'after a discussion' the motion was once more put, and was *lost* by 59 votes to 48. Presumably this was a vote taken by a show of hands, and the meeting was by no means representative of the district. It was left to a non-Park resident to ensure that a poll should take place.[2]

The public meeting took place on 25th March 1885. The Park Trust Committee must have been ready to go into action for on 28th March 1885 a pamphlet was issued to all Park residents exhorting them to vote for incorporation. Its text included the safeguard clause, and pointed out clearly the strategic role that the Park dwellers had played as a group through the committee, able to veto the move, and that to ensure later protection the Park should vote for incorporation on these terms. The precise wording was:

Referring to the instructions given to them by the General Annual Meeting, the Committee think it right to direct the attention of the owners of property,

---

[1] Both lived in Victoria Park.

[2] 'A poll was demanded by Mr. Francis Hampson' (solicitor, Platt Cottage, Rusholme).

and residents in the Park, to the following clause which the Manchester Corporation are willing to insert in their City Extension Bill. (Then followed Clause 5, see p. 37).

Having received an assurance from the Local Board that they refuse to be incorporated with Manchester in case that clause is not passed without alteration, the committee recommend both overseers and occupiers in Victoria Park to vote in favour of Incorporation.

By Order,
E. B. NORTON,
Hon. Sec.[1]

There is no mention of the date of poll in the Board of Health Minute books, but the result was received officially by the Manchester Council and is recorded as such. The Deputy Town Clerk reported the result of the Poll in Rusholme as follows:

In favour of Incorporation	896
Against	465
	431

So the Park dwellers were able to maintain their independence and privacy, despite the ominous growth of the city. It is impossible to say whether the substantial minority against incorporation was dividing along party lines, or how many of them lived in the Park. It is unlikely that this local issue was a factor in local party politics, which were only just beginning to be a matter of party concern.[2] Prominent members of both parties lived in the Park, and outside it. In particular, the broad tract of country that stretched into Fallowfield was occupied by the declining Liberal connection. From the point of view of internal administration some ratepayers, and certainly H. T. Crofton, must have realized that subtler issues were at stake, namely, the very status of the Park Committee itself. Not since the 1836 Act had there been any legal recognition of the Park. The clause in the Extension Act could provide such a recognition, and some precedent as to the status of the highways. In fact it was possible to claim later[3] that the roads were mere footpaths. Crofton, later in the letter quoted above, was able to write gloatingly:

... it was important in view of the question as to what is the Park and how far the Victoria Park Act has any force, that we should obtain a dictum that our roads are mere footpaths. Talbot[4] (not knowing our reasons, or at any rate not stating them, but probably thinking of section 150 of the Public Health Act 1875) consented, and we considered the clause in the light of a Magna Carta.

Crofton need not have been so jubilant—for the Council absolved

---

[1] A copy of this notice is preserved in the Bosdin Leech papers.
[2] See introduction, p. 6. [3] Petition to the Lords, 1920.
[4] Town Clerk, Manchester.

itself of the cost of road maintenance *within* the Park while levying the standard rate from all occupiers inside the area. This was satisfactory while the residents were well-to-do and labour was cheap. But in later years, clause 48 proved to be a burden which the residents would gladly have relinquished, but which the Corporation was by no means eager to share.

CHAPTER IV

SIR WILLIAM ANSON AND THE
BREAKING OF THE BUILDING TIE, 1899

This chapter deals with the legal controversies and the ensuing agreements between the Trust Committee and certain individuals, particularly Sir William Anson, Bt., and groups, which resulted in the breaking of the so-called 'building tie', and the erection of some 650 two- and three-storey terraced houses on the grid-iron pattern in the eastern half of the Park. The Park was, even at the turn of the century, becoming an island of green in the expanding city. As early as 1850 strips of cottages had appeared on its southern side, while the 1870s and 1880s had witnessed the large-scale terraced building to the north of Plymouth Grove.[1] From the legal point of view, though the general outcome is easy to establish, certain points of detail remain obscure, mainly because of the reluctance of counsel to commit themselves on points of detail, and the absence of information about the *personalities* who were actually involved in the transactions. Most of the information is derived from legal briefs which give only opinions as to what the facts were at various stages. At the time, the Trust Committee was in an ambiguous position, and very little appears in the minute books to reveal how their view of their legal position changed. Naturally, Sir William Anson did not wish to reveal more than was necessary of his position, and there is very scant information concerning the other parties.[2]

Basically, two factors were involved in the question of whether cottages[3] should be built in the Park. First, in 1873[4] property which lay within the Park area passed by inheritance to the owner of the property outside but adjacent to the Park, on its southern boundary. The property in question was the Birch estate, part of which had been part of the original scheme of 1836, but which had never been resold when the company passed out of existence in 1845,[5] and had passed to Sir William Anson through the Dickenson family. Secondly, Sir William Anson was not connected with Manchester socially, and probably knew nothing of Victoria Park and its local setting.

The first mention of the matter in the Trust Committee Minute books is on 16th February 1898, when the 'Hon. Sec. read a letter

[1] See map 3.
[2] E.g. there is only one mention of Dr. Bradley, 'one of the proposed purchasers'.
[3] Cottages are terraced 'two up—two down' houses.
[4] See p. 44.   [5] See chap. I, p. 18.

from Mr. W. Kessler,[1] pointing out that information had reached him with regard to the proposed erection of cottages on vacant land at the back of his father's house. A long discussion followed and finally the following resolution was passed:

That Mr. Dunderdale be hereby instructed to make such investigation as he may think fit into the rights which exist (if any) to prevent the building of house property in Victoria Park, of a less annual rent value than £50 and that he was to endeavour to ascertain what obstructions can be made to prevent carriage entrances being effected from vacant land into the Park roads . . .'

At this stage, the precise extent of Sir William's land was not known, neither was how much property he had resold, nor the terms of sale of any such transaction, and whether at this stage an actual scheme to build was projected. It *is* clear that the Trust Committee did not know precisely who owned which land. It appears that Dunderdale was unable to obtain any plans of the exact limits of Sir William's property in the Park, and in the end had to ask Sir William himself for them. To his request, the noted lawyer and Warden of All Souls took a justifiable, though somewhat high-handed, attitude: 'If your clients think that they have any cause for complaint against me, they should state what it is, and not ask me to supply them with materials on which they may wish to found such a case.'[2] That the position was far from clear, and that the Committee was far from confident, may be judged by Sir William's words. He wrote,[3] 'Up to now, you have informed me that certain persons who you do not name allege certain rights which you do not describe, to interfere with my control over a certain portion of my property. On the strength of this information you call upon me to send you a plan of my estate. The request is so extraordinary that I can hardly regard it as serious.'

The position becomes a little clearer when, in a brief to counsel dated 22nd March 1898, the Committee were able to admit that land had been sold, and that there was a definite intention to build cottages. The Committee had sought the opinion of Charles Druce, solicitor, and set out its position with a view to preventing the building of cottages, and possibly to preventing entrance by the building contractors. The case presented described in considerable detail the origin and objects of the original scheme, stressing the intention of the owners to maintain privacy and land values. The crux of the issue was contained in the following words,

It has lately come to the notice of the Victoria Park Trust Committee that the vacant land space between Daisy Bank Road and Anson Road has been purchased by a man who has signified his intention of erecting cottages

---

[1] Of 'Summerville', Daisy Bank Road.
[2] Bosdin Leech MSS, letter dated 6th March, 1898.   [3] *Ibid.*

thereon. The building of these cottages will undoubtedly tend to depreciate the value of the property in Victoria Park, and the Committee are exceedingly anxious to prevent the carrying out of the project if possible. A letter has been written by the solicitors of the builder who has purchased the land, expressing his intention of building cottages thereon, and also demanding that the gates of the various entrances to Victoria Park shall be thrown open forthwith ... it is conceived that if the land owners can prevent the roads being used by the contractor for the purpose of carrying building materials, they may abandon their proposals.

Unfortunately for the Park Committee, part of one of the Park gates lay on the land which had passed to the builder. The question whether he had the right to remove this gate was therefore also to be decided. The Committee also wanted to know 'whether a combination of the owners of land on either side of the respective gates could effect the exclusion of the builders' carts from the Park roads, and counsel is requested to advise the Committee generally on their position in the circumstances outlined above'.

The Committee, though confident of the intentions conceived at the time of the building scheme, felt it was in a weak position as to the lasting applicability of the tie itself:

In all conveyances throughout the whole area of the Park, there was a building tie of £40 p.a., but there was no general Deed to be signed by the purchsers of land, ... and the Vendors do not appear to have entered into any corresponding covenants with the purchasers with regard to land left unbuilt upon. Under the circumstances, it is conceived that it will not be possible to prevent Sir William Anson from breaking the building tie on land adjoining that sold by his predecessor in title.[1]

Whilst careful to indicate the brevity of the information given, Druce was not at all confident that the facts of the case justified confidence on the part of the Trust Committee. In particular, he stated, 'I think that the case is hopeless unless the owners of some land in the Park bought under what is called "a tie", can succeed in making out that through some contract or implied obligation, Sir William Anson became bound by a similar tie in respect of his land.'[2] On the question of the rights of way into the Park, he wrote, 'No doubt the purchasers of land in the Park must have acquired rights of way over them by usage, if not by express grant, but I do not see why they should not be proved to belong to Sir William Anson, in the same way as the rest of the unsold[3] land.' The matter was that if building was possible, then transport to and from the building sites was possible, therefore Druce finally suggested more

---

[1] Thus, at this stage, it is clear that the Committee believed that both Sir William Anson and another were about to build.
[2] It is Sir William whose right is always challenged: it is therefore possible that he sold the land on chief rent to the builder.
[3] 'Unsold' by the original company, and therefore reconveyed to Sir William's predecessors.

careful enquiry into the circumstances of the purchases of land by persons whose interests were now threatened, to see if a case can possibly be made out to support an injunction against Sir William Anson's purchaser.

THE INHERITANCE OF THE BIRCH ESTATE

John Dickenson (1689–1779) purchased Birch Estate, 1745

↓

John Dickenson (1726–1810)

↓

John Dickenson (1752–1842) sold land to the promoters of the Victoria Park scheme; the land was reconveyed in 1839

↓

Louise Francis Dickenson,
      (only child)   m. 1845 to General Sir William Anson

↓

Sir John William Hamilton Anson (1816–1873)

↓

Sir William Anson, Bt. (1843–1914) M.P., Warden of All Souls (in conflict with the Victoria Park Trust Committee on the 'building tie' question)

See 'The Dickensons of Birch' in Buckley, *The History of Birch-in-Rusholme*, chap. II.

Dunderdale reported this advice to the Committee, who instructed him to prepare a further case, which went into considerably more detail. He attempted to show that the original building tie still applied to all property in the Park. Thus, John Dickenson[1] was the original owner of all the land in question. From various titles, it is shown that the land was conveyed by Dickenson for the purpose of building and that a tie of in no case lower than £40 per house was insisted upon by the terms of the covenants. It now appeared that there were three parcels of the original Dickenson land, one of which remained with Sir William. 'The title of one portion is found to come from Dickenson through Joseph Denison successively to the present owners—another portion is found to come from Westhead, also from John Dickenson ... and mentioned in the Victoria Park Act—the remaining portion of the land is derived from Sir William Anson as the heir at law and successor in title to the Dickenson Estates.' All the present owners intended to build

---

[1] The predecessor of Sir William Anson—see chart of the inheritance of the estate above.

cottages 'of a very much lower rental'. The Committee, however, claimed that

from a comparison of the title deeds and plans, it has been ascertained that in all the titles adjoining the land in question covenants with ties similar to the covenants hereinbefore mentioned are contained, and it is the fact that the whole of the houses which have been erected upon the land in this district have been built in accordance with these terms, and it has always been commonly understood that such tie existed, and that each landowner was precluded from erecting houses upon the land, below the value specified. . . .

Despite these ostensibly stronger claims made by Dunderdale on behalf of the Trust Committee, Druce had to point out the fundamental weakness of the Trust's position. In the first place, 'It would be going too far to say that there is any proof of his [John Dickenson] ever having promulgated any scheme for building on his own individual account.' The absence of any mutual agreement between residents adjoining the land in question meant that 'all that one can look to is what right any one owner can make out in the special circumstances'.

What you want is some one person who will come forward as a plaintiff and who can prove that he or someone through whom he derives his title purchased his land from a former owner of the land now meant to be built upon, and conveyed in express terms, that all the adjoining land, including that meant to be now built upon, was to be bound by a similar restriction. I fear that unless someone can be found who is able to make out a case such as I have described above, it will be impossible to prevent the building of the cottages.

This brief is dated 7th June 1898.

At a meeting on 8th June 1898 the Hon. Sec. of the Park Committee reported the unfavourable opinion that Mr. Druce had given, and also the efforts that he had been making to obtain evidence for a second case to lay before counsel in London. It came out that one Park resident could claim that 'the property on which his land was built had been purchased on the condition that the land behind it should not be built upon, except with a tie of £40'. The committee therefore decided that 'additional enquiries from various people were necessary to see if it was possible to find someone who could directly allege that he bought his land on the express undertaking that the adjoining land was not to be built upon except with a tie'.

Although it was not possible to find any such persons, 'owing mainly to the lapse of 60 years since the properties were conveyed', a further glimmer of hope was seen at a meeting specially called to consider the question on 23rd June 1898.[1] Edward Guthrie,[2] the chairman of the Trust, reported 'that he had been approached by

---

[1] Trust Committee minutes.   [2] See p. 52.

Dr. Bradley, one of the purchasers, with a view to selling the plot to the Trust Committee'. As a result of this announcement, a small executive committee was appointed 'to confer with the purchasers with regard to the whole question'.

The purchasers (they are still not named) must have realized the strength of their position, for on 9th July 1898 a further special meeting was held, when the negotiations between the sub-committee and the purchasers of the land were described during which 'the members of the sub-committee were informed that they had until Friday next to purchase the land in question for £21,500'. A meeting of all owners and residents was called for 14th July, and a circular was printed, 'pointing out to the ratepayers in what manner their interests had been protected'. There is unfortunately no record in the minutes of this meeting, or of the circular, but it is clear that the committee were seriously divided, probably over the question of how the money could be raised. At the following meeting on 20th July 1898 'letters from Messrs. Salomonson, Smith and Wren were read to the meeting, in reference to the building scheme and the replies he had sent disclosed to the meeting. It was resolved that a letter of regret be written to Mr. Wren and that he be asked to consider his resignation from the Trust.'[1]

At this stage in the negotiations, yet another case was laid before a London Q.C., Oliver Glen. The situation was now further complicated by Sir William Anson's attempt, in his capacity as owner of the Birch estate, which lay to the south of the Park, to call in question the right of the Park Committee to prevent access to the area at the toll gate. It seems certain that Anson's 'threat'[2] was an attempt to force the Committee's hand. In addition, he probably anticipated the intention of the Committee to question the legality of his contract with the builder, implicitly disregarding the tie.

For the most part, this fresh case added little to the former in so far as the building tie was concerned. It was admitted that

it would appear that there is no chance of preventing Sir William Anson from carrying out his contract with the builder, which, it is understood, involves the sale of chief or ground rents together with a release of the building tie, but Counsel is requested to advise the Committee whether he thinks it would be possible to make out a case for an injunction against Sir William Anson, from entering into contract or against the builders, restraining him from building in accordance with his avowed object.

The brief goes on to explain

that the main reason for the submission of this case is in order to ascertain the rights of Sir William Anson as owner of land on the outskirts of Victoria Park, as well as those of the other owners within the Park area, as regards the continued existence of the gates and with regard to the levying of tolls.

<hr />

[1] Minutes.   [2] See p. 42.

It has come to the knowledge of the Trust Committee that Sir William Anson has declared that the existence of Victoria Park with its gates is a serious detriment to his property which lies outside the Park area to the south of Dickenson Road, and that he intends, one of these days, if occasion should require, to have the gates removed by force.

The question was whether the Park residents, through the agency of the Trust Committee, owned the gates, and could thus prevent Sir William Anson from 'carrying out his threatened purposes'.

Advice was sought chiefly on the following points:

(i) The possibility of preventing Sir William Anson from completing his contract,

(ii) the rights of Victoria Park Trust Committee in regard to the maintenance of gates and lodges,

(iii) the rights of the owners of land on which the owners of gates and lodges are situate,

(iv) the possibility of removing the gates to other positions,

(v) the right of a possible syndicate to set up new gates,

(vi) the rights of the owners of land on which gates lie, should Anson remove the gates by force, and

(vii) the rights to levy tolls and tolls according to the weight of vehicles passing through.

The possibility of preventing any contract was expressly denied by Counsel. It was pointed out that even if the building tie was thoroughly established, the erection of cottages of less than £40 unless expressly required, 'would be the act of the purchaser, and not that of the vendor'. Stipulating the similarity of covenant, Counsel was able to advise that 'any of the other land owners who deduce their title from the company may enforce that covenant against a person proceeding to build on the land in question. . . .'

On (ii) counsel was of the opinion that any owner of property inside the Park could not prevent the closing of the gates to prevent the passing of carts, since the Committee maintained the gates by permission of the owners of soil on which the gates stood. On (iii) the opinion of Counsel was that owners of soil on which gates and lodges stood were not obliged to maintain them. Both the removal and the setting up of new gates was permissible in Counsel's opinion. On (vi) should Anson remove the gates by force, then it was believed that the owners of land on which the gates stood would have rights of action against him for trespass. Finally, the right to levy tolls was, in the opinion of Mr. Glen, unquestionable.[1]

This, then, was the position: land, which had originally belonged to Dickenson, had been sold to two parties at the time of the formation of the Victoria Park Company. For the purposes of the Company a building tie had been agreed of not less than £40 p.a. These

[1] Counsel's opinion, 7th June 1898.

parcels of land, however, were reconveyed to Westhead and Denison, from whom they passed to the present owners, who intended to put up cottages. Successive owners had not expressly required the building tie on land adjacent to their own. All three owners had sold land to persons who intended to build cottages. Sir William Anson also was claiming the right to remove the Anson Road gate.[1] It does not seem to be the case that Anson sold *all* the land to builders. Two other parties were also responsible. Anson had succeeded to the Birch Estate in 1873[2] and initiated the move in 1898. Why such a move was made just then, except that the demand for houses was rising,[3] remains obscure. Counsel had advised the Trust that its control of tolls was unquestionable, but that in the absence of express statements in recent covenants of land adjoining the sold land, it was almost certain that the building could not be prevented. Nor is this surprising in view of the lapse of time since the company which perpetrated the tie had been formed and unofficially dissolved.[4]

Eventually, the matter was settled by agreement between all the parties concerned, but in the meantime 'a letter was received from Messrs. Wadsworth and Son, as agents for the Woodhead Trustees, in relation to the existence of a gate across the Dickenson Road end of Anson Road which, it was alleged, materially interfered with the development of their property and right of way'.[5]

The Committee replied to this by placing the gate under toll and stated that, should the Woodhead Trustees remove the gate, then legal action would be taken. Sometime in late October 1898 the gate must have been removed, for on 9th November 1898 it was moved 'that proceedings be taken against the Woodhead Trustees, by reason of the removal of the Dickenson Road gate, such proceedings to be taken by Mr. Harvey Goodwin[6] on behalf of himself, and other owners and tenants in the Park'.

The question of the cottage building was settled out of court by the formation of the Victoria Park, Manchester, Land Company. It has not been possible to discover the precise details of the formation of this company. The *London Gazette* of 20th January 1914 contains the usual bald statement, reporting its liquidation. The liquidator was Thomas Bazley, and the meeting was at the offices of A. & C. W. Fox, the solicitors to the Trust Committee. The centenary booklet states that the Company 'acquired the land in question and thus prevented the cottages being built, and an agreement was made

---

[1] 'The gate [situated at the extreme southern end of Anson Road] had up to this point been kept locked, certain owners alone having keys, for there was then no through traffic along Anson Road' (A *Short Account of the Victoria Park*, p. 20).
[2] Buckley, *History of Birch-in-Rusholme*, p. 21.
[3] See ch. IV, p. 42.   [4] See ch. I, p. 16.
[5] Minutes, 20th October 1898.
[6] The owner of the other half of the gate.

on 19th September 1899 between the Trust, this Company and the Woodhead Trustees which settled the question. The cottages were not built but a number of new streets and small houses were built in the eastern portion of the Park according to road plans prepared by the Land Company'. Who owned this company, whether individuals in private capacity, or as representatives of the Trust Committee, is uncertain. Three of the directors who signed a second agreement concerning the Dickenson Road gate were C. H. Arning, who lived at Brook House, Oxford Place, William Kessler, who lived at 'Summerville', Daisy Bank Road (Trust Chairman 1900–1909), and W. E. Gromme, who was later to become treasurer to the Trust 1911–30, and who lived in Lower Park Road. Only Kessler had land near to the proposed cottages.

The question of the toll gate was also settled by agreement. In January 1899 the whole question was discussed thoroughly:

Mr. Wadsworth, (the representative of the Woodhead Trustees) was present and was requested by the Chairman to explain his views with regard to the situation. After considerable discussion, in which it appeared that there was really little in dispute, it was then proposed that a meeting be arranged between Mr. Wadsworth, the Victoria Park Trust Committee and the Victoria Park Land Company to work for a settlement of the question.[1]

Despite this promise of settlement, Sir William Anson, as owner of property inside and outside the Park, continued to press his claim to remove the gates. Again Druce was consulted, and he was of the opinion that the gate would have to be opened[2] as far as Anson was concerned, but that it was quite clear that the gate could not be thrown open to the public (opinion dated 17th February 1899).

At the following meeting of the Trust Committee it was resolved 'that Mr. Arning, Mr. Kessler and Mr. Dunderdale be appointed a committee to wait upon Sir William Anson at Oxford with full power to make what arrangements they thought fit in regard to the controversy . . .'[3] These negotiations went well, for on 30th June 1899 Sir William wrote to the Secretary:

I have thought over the question of the gates on Anson Road and have come to the conclusion that if those who live on the Birch Estate have free access to and from Manchester for themselves, and persons dealing with them, I should be willing not to press my right to have the gate removed. I should ask that the gates stand open and that the notice be altered so as to include my entire property in the privilege claimed by the Victoria Park Trust for the inhabitants of the Park.

A further agreement was made between the Victoria Park Trust, Harvey Goodwin, and the Land Company. This agreement provided that a toll gate should be erected and maintained at the

---

[1] Minutes, 25 January 1899.   [2] I.e. on non-payment of tolls.
[3] Minutes, 22nd February 1899.

expense of the Trust, that the gates may be removed by either party on twelve months' notice, and that building materials could enter the Park by that gate free of charge.

It has been described in another place[1] how, after 1900, many of the older houses, as they became vacant, passed not to fresh private tenants, but were taken over for institutional residence. The change had set in. Although people continued to refer to the Park as a rural retreat, the days of a country aspect were now demonstrably over, and the Park Committee, representing a gradually dwindling and, after 1914, an ever more apathetic set of local notables found it increasingly difficult to defend the privacy of the area.

[1] See Chap. V, pp. 57–59.

PLATE 1 Saville House/Stonywood/Ward Hall, Lower Park Road.

PLATE 2 Unitarian College, Summerville, Daisy Bank Road (c. 1904).

PLATE 3 Summerville, another view.

PLATE 4 Westerfield, Park Crescent, Victoria Park, Cobden's last Manchester residence.

PLATE 5 Richard Lane's house, Oxford Lodge.

PLATE 6   Ivy Villa, Upper Park Road.

PLATE 7 Ivy Villa, later view prior to demolition.

PLATE 8   Ivy Villa, the south side, corner of Upper Park Road and Denison Road.

PLATE 9   Regent House/Marylands, Lower Park Road.

PLATE 10 The Gables, Hope Road.

PLATE 11 Terraced houses, Laindon Road.

PLATE 12   Carolside, from the south, Upper Park Road.

CHAPTER V

SOCIAL BACKGROUND, 1880–1940

The remaining chapters of this book will be concerned with a detailed analysis of the arrangements which the Park Committee made with the local authority, in order to attempt to preserve what remained of the privacy and seclusion of the area. In the introduction the social and economic background from 1838 to 1860 was sketched, and this chapter will attempt to do the same for the remaining period. This, it is suggested, will throw into the relief of the changing urban scene the detailed negotiations and agreements which form the main body of the monograph.

It would be difficult to establish in great detail, but it seems fairly clear from the initial enquiry that has been made that the last quarter of the nineteenth century was becoming more dominated by larger organizations and by the professional servants of these organizations. In the city of Manchester this trend is illustrated by the incorporation of the surrounding townships, and the emergence of a group of professional people whose lives were intimately connected with the emerging educational institutions. These men, as had done their business predecessors, permeated all local groups and cliques, political parties and professional associations. Of course, they depended for support on a flourishing business community scattered through the still expanding suburbs. But they set the tone for the period; it is they if anyone who are the dominant type, and who occupy the key positions. They were the new experts in law and science, in touch with complexities of the era of technical expertise now clearly emerging.

Even accepting that this period can be delineated as clearly as suggested, there are bound to be particular examples which do not fit. In political terms, perhaps the man who spans the two periods which Whitaker distinguishes as the personality-dominated and the organization-dominated, is John Slagg,[1] who lived in the Park from 1861 to 1882. His father had been an active Liberal, and a companion of Cobden. The son, born in 1841, became a director of the Chamber of Commerce when only twenty-three. He was an active member of that successful institution,[2] the Manchester Liberal Association. He was President of the Chamber of Commerce, hon. secretary of the Athenaeum, and M.P. for Manchester from 1879

---

[1] *Manchester Guardian*, 3rd March 1875; 3rd May 1889 (obituary).
[2] Whitaker, p. 68.

to 1885. He has been described as 'one of those leading men of this period who worked [for the Liberals] without any great publicity or adulation'.[1] In politics, the change from personal to professional dominance, to which reference has been made, meant the change-over from a restricted electorate, dominated by well-known local figures, to a mass electorate, organized by professional politicians and party servants. So far as the Liberals were concerned,[2] this found expression in 1874, in the abandonment of the practice of publishing long lists of committees, and replacing these by a small committee of three for the candidature of John Bright. Slagg was one of this new school of Liberal politicians and was a member of this 1874 Committee.

Turning to the new professional men proper, locally and of immediate relevance, such men as Roscoe,[3] Hopkinson,[4] Donner,[5] Guthrie[6] and Darbishire[7] stand out, and are mentioned as residents of the area in question. Roscoe's connection with the creation of the leading chemistry teaching school in the country is well known. He had been schooled in Germany by Bunsen, and came to the chair at Manchester when only twenty-seven. For his services on the Royal Commission on Technical Education he was knighted in 1884. In 1885 he was the Liberal candidate for South Manchester and defeated Thomas Sowler in 1886.[8] He played a prominent part in the promotion of the Technical Education Acts, 1888–89. As Whitaker puts it, 'a resident of Victoria Park, he was typical of the Liberal-professional men of the area'.[9] The arrival of these men socially, as well as politically, was demonstrated when Roscoe was chosen as President of the then newly formed South Manchester Liberal Association in 1886. This marked the beginning of a period of

[1] Whitaker, p. 68.

[2] Once more, generalization is made difficult by lack of research into the growth of the Manchester Conservatives.

[3] Henry Roscoe (1833–1915), *Manchester Guardian*, 20th December 1915; his own *Life and Times*; W. H. Chaloner, *The Movement for the Extension of Owens College, Manchester, 1863–73*, 1973; English MSS, 963–964 (his correspondence with Gladstone), John Rylands University Library, Manchester.

[4] Alfred Hopkinson (1851–1939), *Times*, 13th November 1939; his own *Penultima*.

[5] Edward Donner (1840–1934), *Manchester Guardian*, 31st December 1934.

[6] Edward Guthrie (1841–1904), *Manchester Guardian*, 22nd August 1904 (obituary). He lived in the Park 1876–1904. Guthrie, as an accountant of outstanding ability, added a further dimension to the power that these professional men derived from their expert knowledge: '. . . as the chairman of the Finance Committee of the Lancs. County Council, he was practically the Lancs. Chancellor'. He was a chairman of the Manchester Liberal Union, and chairman of the special committee that drafted the constitution of the 1903 Manchester Liberal Federation. He was consulting accountant to the unsuccessful Association for the Amalgamation of Salford and Manchester, and was practically responsible for the bringing together of the municipalities in 1888. He assisted in the formation of the Manchester Society of Chartered Accountants, and lived at Albert Villa, 1876–1882, and at Milverton Lodge from 1882 to 1904.

[7] Robert Dukinfield Darbishire (1829–1908), *City News*, 4th April 1908.

[8] See above, introduction, pp. 7–8.   [9] Thesis, p. 80.

domination of Liberal politics by this clique, which Whitaker cites as one cause of the final debacle of the party locally by about 1900. Roscoe prospered greatly. He lived modestly in Park Crescent, close to the Rusholme entrance, from 1864 to 1870, removing thence to a newly-built house along Upper Park Road. He remained here till 1885, when he emigrated to Fallowfield.

Edward Donner, whose period in the Park corresponds almost identically with Roscoe's, provides a hybrid case between the merchant–politician and the professional-man–politician, for 'though he eventually gave himself to the life of a merchant, his academic career was one of some distinction'. He won an open scholarship to Oxford, and took a first in Mods. His name occurs frequently as one of that powerful set of South Manchester Liberals, but he was also very active in the formation of the University, being elected to the Court in 1873. He was President of the South Manchester Liberal Association in 1885, and succeeded Sir Charles Swann as President of the Manchester Liberal Association in 1907. He, with R. D. Darbishire, was active in the promotion of the Manchester High School for Girls.[1] He lived in Park Crescent from 1863 to 1875, when he moved to Anson Road, until 1888, after which he followed Roscoe into Fallowfield.

The lawyer, R. D. Darbishire, though apparently an individualist to a marked degree, also provides an example of those men who came to dominate the Park and the area during the last quarter of the nineteenth century. Once more there is the close connection with the foundation of Owens College and the Victoria University.[2] He was, for example, one of a committee of six appointed to raise money for the extension fund and played a major role in the Parliamentary negotiations for the extension of the College. His connection with the Girls' High School has been mentioned. He was also one of the three trustees appointed to dispose of the Whitworth fortune, and took an active interest in the gallery provided from that legacy.

Sir Alfred Hopkinson was probably the last of the great professional Liberals. His years as a resident of Victoria Park were wholly in the twentieth century, though he is clearly very typical of the genre already mentioned. His lineage was pure Manchester, his father John, born in Cheetham Hill in 1823, was again a Liberal of the old school, playing a prominent role in local politics. He was councillor for St. Luke's Ward in 1861, Alderman from 1872, and Mayor in 1882–83. He was an engineer of tremendous energy, selling and installing cotton machinery all over Europe during the middle years of the century. At the time of Alfred's birth the family were living in Rumford Street, Chorlton-on-Medlock, whence they moved to York Place, then Grove House and finally out to Bowdon.

[1] Burstall, p. 38.   [2] Thompson, pp. 242, 259, 309–10.

Alfred, one of a family of five sons and four daughters, most of whom led distinguished professional careers, was educated locally[1] at a private school, and at Owens College, which had then not left Quay Street. From 1869 to 1872 he was at Lincoln College under Mark Pattison, and then came back to Manchester as Professor of Law. In 1889 he resigned his chair for practice as a Q.C. in London. From 1897 to 1913 he was again in Manchester, and from 1900 was Vice-Chancellor of the University. During these years he lived in Victoria Park. Like the other professionals he was interested in politics. In 1885, for example, he had unsuccessfully opposed Balfour for the East Manchester seat. After 1886 he became a leading local Liberal-Unionist. Professionally, he witnessed 'a mighty expansion of the University and the addition of new faculties and new professorships, session by session'. He was an intellectual Liberal,[2] almost the antithesis of his political predecessors who dwelt in the neighbourhood, with their almost religious conviction that the tenets of the Free Trade philosophy were just and true.

The last quarter of the nineteenth century, then, is marked by the beginning of the emergence of those tendencies which were later to change the whole function of the area. The local symptoms of the growth of a professional society have already been hinted at. By the 1880s the professional men,[3] as well as the merchants, were building new property in the Park. The procession of occupation which had been so characteristic of the early and middle years of the century, that is, from Greenheys, Oxford Road and Plymouth Grove, was now beginning to extend itself out into Fallowfield, Didsbury, Withington and beyond. During the 1850s and 1860s Fallowfield began to be extensively developed. The circular railway lines through Withington and Fallowfield were opened in 1880 and 1891–92 respectively. Central Station became 'fashionable'.[4] Around the Park itself, by the 1880s urban sprawl was already in evidence. Much of the land to the north and east was now covered with terraced property (see map 4). Those institutions which were to become so characteristic of the twentieth century phase of the area's history were already entering the region. In 1870 the Roman Catholic Industrial School was built, and ten years later, Dalton Hall was erected.[5] In 1877, too, a Methodist College was put up just north of the Crescent at the Rusholme end.

[1] Dr. Adams's School, 'Eaglesfield', Victoria Park.

[2] He wrote, *Rebuilding Britain—a survey of the problems of Reconstruction*, 1917.

[3] E.g. Roscoe built 'Firwood', Professor A. S. Wilkins built 'Wood Lea', and the architect, Edward Salomons, built two houses, 'Hirstwood' and 'The Gables', which he occupied successively for a number of years.

[4] See W. C. Williamson, *Sketches of Fallowfield*, 1888. Alfred Waterhouse, the famous architect, built his house in Fallowfield in 1861 (Stewart, *Stones of Manchester*).

[5] Dalton Hall, founded in 1876 in Greenheys, was erected in the Park between 1880 and 1882 (G. A. Sutherland, *Dalton Hall: a Quaker venture*, 1963).

All these developments, in their indirect ways, reflect those characteristics of a growing urban society, the emergence of a professional class, and the large-scale organization, educating its members and housing them in specialized temporary accommodation. Effectively, 1900 marked the real beginning of this new phase of institutional residence and recuperative accommodation, for it was in this year that R. D. Darbishire bought 'Ashburne House'[1] which had been the home of W. R. Callender, jun., and gave it to the University, to be used as a women's hall of residence. Among those who had promoted this scheme were many of those leading Liberals and professionals, such as Donner, Hopkinson and Professor A. S. Wilkins.[2]

After 1900 both the settlement of the building tie question[3] and the inflationary and secular rise in rents meant that the old restriction on building inside the Park was gone. In any case, the building of the 'slums of the Park'[4] meant the end of the age of the large detached property, standing in its own grounds.[5] The immediate result of the removal of the building tie, was the erection of some 650 two- and three-storied terraced houses, and closely packed semi-detached houses, along some dozen or so streets on the grid-iron plan.[6] This rapid development can be seen forming a part of conurbation-wide activity, for it was during the same period, i.e. 1895–1910, that the rate of house building in Manchester doubled, compared with the previous four years.[7] It was during this period, too, that Trafford Park Estate began to develop. These new properties were occupied for the most part by what was probably the lower section of that professional class, some of whose leading members are mentioned above. The tables on page 56 show an occupation analysis for some of the new streets.

It was during these pre-1914 years, too, that the large semi-detached houses along Daisy Bank Road were put up, opposite Stafford House, combining some of the neo-Tudor features of which Salomons had made such ample use some twenty-five years or so earlier.

Very little building went on during the period 1910–20, either in Park or city. After 1920 building in Manchester was patchy and

[1] Marked 'Egerton Hall' on the 1922 map.

[2] The gradual permeation of the area by this type of accommodation, which marks the final phase of the Park's social development; is dealt with below, pp. 57–60.

[3] See Chap. V. pp. 41–50.

[4] A phrase used in private correspondence by Miss Nora Zeigler, in 1960 one of the few remaining survivors of the pre-1900 era, to describe the new terraces put up in the eastern half of the Park. Her grandfather bought 'Lily Villa' in 1865. Her father took over the house and family business in 1886.

[5] The last house of this type to go up was Chadlington House, 1914.

[6] See map 6.

[7] From 1891–95 the rate was 750 p.a., 1895–1910 the rate rose to 1900. (H. Rees, *A Growth Map for Manchester*; J. S. McConechy 'The economic value of the Manchester Ship Canal', *Trans. Manchester Statistical Society*, 1912.)

TABLE ONE
CURZON AVENUE

1904	*1912*
2 solicitors	1 solicitor
2 engineers	1 merchant
1 cashier	3 travellers
1 bank clerk	1 manufacturer
1 chemist	1 buyer
1 pattern card maker	1 architect
1 fruiterer	1 jeweller
3 unknown*	1 science lecturer
	1 photographer
	1 secretary
	1 commission agent
	1 bank clerk
	7 unknown*

TABLE TWO
KENSINGTON AVENUE

1904	*1912*
3 managers	1 teacher
1 clerk	1 salesman
2 travellers	1 engineer
1 inspector	1 fish merchant
1 supervisor	12 unknown*

TABLE THREE
LANGDALE ROAD, 1908

2 teachers	3 salesmen	1 traveller
2 cashiers	1 stock-keeper	1 printer's reader
5 clerks	1 accountant	1 cutter
1 surveyor	1 manager	1 fruiterer
1 yarn agent	2 warehousemen	1 pawnbroker
1 book-keeper	13 unknown*	1 clothier
1 inspector		1 draper

*Research into occupations through street directories is made difficult since the more recent street directories give no house address with the business address, and not always the occupation with the home address.

sporadic.[1] The suburbs of Didsbury and Withington, which in 1914 had been suburban villages, were joined on to the city by new housing and playing fields.[2] The new suburbs were evidently being occupied by people moving from regions further towards the centre

[1] Rees, *op. cit.*, p. 14.
[2] Freeman, *Conurbations of Great Britain*, p. 139; L. P. Green, *Provincial Metropolis*, pp. 74–5.

of the city. Inside the Park itself, development reflected precisely what was happening outside. The characteristic dwelling was not now the 'weighty terrace', but the 'modern semi', laid out in rows or culs-de-sac, as if they had somehow become detached from the estates to the south and drifted north to settle in little pockets in the no man's land of the Park. Most of this building went on in the 1930s, principal developments being Redclyffe Avenue (1933), the streets of Longford Place (1935) and Crescent Range about 1937. After the war there were several isolated houses of this type erected, notably along Daisy Bank Road and Conyngham Road, and more recently further blocks of flats have appeared.

In the case of private family residence, then, the example of Victoria Park makes any urban zoning framework completely unrealistic. What in fact has happened here, because of certain administrative and historical factors, has been the imposition over about 130 years of some half-dozen or so 'layers' of private housing, the earliest of which, owing to the broad emergence of a professional and welfare society, have been converted to other purposes. This results today in a highly complex mixture, both socially and architecturally.

Coterminous with this new building was another principal factor of the local changing urban scene, viz. the evacuation of the older type properties, and their conversion to miscellaneous 'services' purposes. It is usual to explain this phenomenon in terms of the migration of the population and functional zones, out from the centre of the city either directly or by the outward movement of a sector which is itself expanding. However, when explaining residential building, detailed examination either obviates the need for such a general framework, or shows such frameworks to be too unrealistic to be applicable.[1] In this particular study the concentration of a particular type of nineteenth-century accommodation, in a small and later isolated area, is to be explained chiefly by historical factors, though it may be true that the Park forms part of a very roughly defined area across South Manchester which exhibits similar characteristics.

Contrary to what one would expect, the year 1900 and not 1918 seems to be the dividing line between the old and the new. It will be remembered that it was in this year that R. D. Darbishire gave the house 'Ashburne' to the University, for conversion into a students' hostel. Even before 1914 there was a rapid increase in the number of schools and halls of residence in the Park. 'Ashburne' added a wing to itself in 1901, and leased a semi-detached house in Dickenson Road in 1906. The connection of the Roman Catholic

[1] Most of the work on urban ecology, particularly attempts to explain in general terms 'patterns' of city development, has been done by Americans.

Church with the area, which is now very strong, began in 1907, when the houses 'Sunbury' and 'Firwood' were taken over from the merchants Kessler and Franks respectively. Two years later, what is now the main building of the Xaverian College was completed as an extension of 'Firwood'. In 1905 the great house 'Summerville' on Daisy Bank Road, which had been the home of William Kessler since 1859, was taken over as a Unitarian College. It was during this pre-1914 period, too, that Hulme Hall (now comprising three houses and their grounds) first came to the Park. In 1907 'Oak Bank' was vacated by the widow of Thomas Sowler.[1] 'Oaklands', next door, became the Fielden School after the death of Henry Salomonson in 1908 and several other schools appeared about this time. Of course, there had always been a high demand for private education[2] in the area, and at least two of the older-type buildings were put up for educational purposes, e.g., Ellerslie College[3] (1861) in Upper Park Road, which was a pioneer institution in women's higher education, and 'Eaglesfield' (1851) in Anson Road, which was built with the help of E. R. Langworthy for O. A. Ferris, who had come to Manchester from London as the tutor to W. R. Callender, jun., in 1838.[4] In 1903 a school was opened at No. 3 Anson Road[5] and there were also schools in Windsor Place, Daisy Bank Road, and in Park Crescent during this period. Nursing homes, too, begin to appear in the directories about this time. The Lingards Home, in Anson Road, and 'Eaglesfield', which had been an annex to Dalton from 1902 to 1912, was converted about 1914. 'High Elms', for many years the home of R. D. Darbishire, also appears in the 1914 directory as a nursing home. It was in or about 1911 that Langdale Hall first became a hostel for women students and in 1919 that Saville House in Lower Park Road was taken over as an overspill for students from 'Summerville', which had been leased from the Unitarians for the war period. It was known as Ward Hall, after the principal of Owens College. There is some evidence, too, that some of the older properties were beginning to be converted into

[1] See page 7.
[2] See Bryce, *Report of Schools Enquiry Commission*, 1864–67.
[3] Ellerslie was run for many years by Miss Anderson. Initially the author assumed that Miss Anderson was connected with the movement for women's higher education in Manchester. However, there is no mention of her or Ellerslie in Sara Burstall's account of the Girls' High School. Bryce wrote: '. . . there is a notion in Manchester that while the Grammar School is the right place for a boy going to the University, a boy intended for business had better be sent to one of the better private schools' (p. 718). It seems that this reflection of the division between the business men and the professional men applied also to the emerging women's institutions. Angela Brazil, for example, the founder of the schoolgirls' story genre, who became head girl of Ellerslie, went to the junior classes at 'the High'. Her father was a cotton merchant who lived successively in Greenheys and Rusholme (*My Own School Days*, 1925).
[4] *City News*, 4th June 1892, (obituary).
[5] Opposite the church.

some form of broken residence. In 1914 'Fairfield', once occupied by Sir Alfred Hopkinson, became a 'guest house' and remained so for about ten years. There was also a boarding house and a students' hostel in Anson Road before 1914.

After 1920 most of the houses that were vacated as family residences were converted into nursing homes. In 1925 the great gothic-type Denison House, in Denison Road, became the Manchester and Salford Nursing Institution; and next door 'Hill View' became the Hill View Nursing Home. In 1926 'Wood Thorpe' on Oxford Place also demolished, appears as a nursing home, and the great house, of 'Sunnyside' on Conyngham Road became St. Mary's in the same year. Opposite, 'Lynfield' appears as a home in 1923. The house standing at the Oxford Road entrance became St. Gabriel's, a hall of residence for women undergraduates, in 1920, while the University quitted Ward Hall in 1922, the building being taken over by the Theosophical Society. During the 1920s the first house along Anson Road (now part of the Manchester Foot Hospital) was known as the Ellerslea School, though whether it merely borrowed the famous old name, or whether it was a continuation, is not clear. In 1922 'Westfield', the second house along Anson Road, became a private hotel.

During the 1930s the tendency was for nursing homes to remain a high proportion of those buildings that had been converted, but for new conversions to be mostly to educational and broken residential institutions. Along Anson Road in 1930 at least nine houses were definitely not being used for private residence. There were three nursing homes, three halls of residence, two annexes to Dalton and one annexe to St. Anselm's, one private hotel, one school and one home for Christian Women Workers (St. Hilda's). In 1936 Anson House appears as 'apartments' and in 1938 the Victoria Park School was displaced by the Lancashire Mental Welfare Centre. Oxford Place changed during this decade. 'Gabs.',[1] of course, remained. The house 'Woodthorpe' was demolished in 1939 to make room for what must have been a block of service flats. The widow of Charles Arning died about 1933 and 'Brook House' was taken over by the M.E.C. Day Trades School for Girls. It became the College for Domestic Science in 1938. In 1934 the Manchester Foot Hospital occupied 'Aulgirth', while the house 'Thornbury' became Brookfield Hotel in 1938. Throughout the decade 'Ashburne' was occupied by the Manchester Theological College.

Along Lower Park Road notable changes were the addition of Regent House to the Xaverian College in 1930 to be used as for novitiates, and the building of a second block of service flats, 'Carfax', in what was formerly the grounds of 'Redclyffe'. It is difficult

[1] St. Gabriel's.

to establish from street directories precisely when some of the houses were cut up into flats, but it seems quite likely from a few inquiries that have been made that some 'guest houses' were appearing about this time. The Sapphire Villa Hotel was built in Park Crescent in 1938.

By the late 1930s then, although some of the older houses were still occupied by private residents, notably along Daisy Bank Road and Anson Road, the character of the area as a private *residential* estate had completely changed, the main function of most of the buildings being institutional in character. Alongside this change it is possible to trace a change in the occupational character of those residents who remained. During the mid-nineteenth century the prominent 'Park-type' had been the merchant. This began to change towards the end of the century, when professional people, teachers, doctors and lawyers, began to be resident in large numbers. This is the period to which Katherine Chorley referred: 'Then, . . . when I was a child, a group of lawyers and doctors and professors still lived in Victoria Park in houses surrounded by gardens.'[1]

[1] *Manchester Made Them*, p. 146.

CHAPTER VI

THE EXCLUSION OF PUBLIC TRANSPORT AND THE ADMISSION OF PRIVATE MOTOR CARS, 1900–1914

Despite the increasing urban aspect of the neighbourhood, the growth of the administrative region of Manchester and the declining number of important local notables living in the Park, the years 1900–14 mark the last period in which the residents, through the Trust Committee, could seriously resist the Corporation. Before 1914 both public and private transport had been revolutionized by the coming of the electric tram and the motor car. The Park made a spirited attempt to exclude the former, which was successful, and a less reasonable attempt to exclude the latter, which was not.

In 1901 the horse-drawn trams were withdrawn from the streets of the city, and replaced by a system of electric trams. In the Manchester City Corporation Bill for 1902 the Corporation proposed to deal with certain tramway matters, which seriously affected the privacy of the Park. Until this time, tramlines had passed along Upper Brook Street and High Street, and at the other end of Anson road, along Dickenson Road, from Wilmslow Road to Stockport Road. The proposal was to continue the line through the Park, along Anson Road, forming a complete circle, and to link Chorlton-on-Medlock to Birchfields. Section 17 of the Bill also proposed 'to repeal, alter or amend the provisions of Section 48 of the Manchester City Extension Act 1885, relating to Victoria Park, Rusholme'.

Early in 1902,[1] at the quarterly committee meeting, 'a communication was read from Mr. Boyle (chairman of the Tramways Committee) to Mr. Andrews, with regard to the possibility of an arrangement being come to for trams to run along Anson Road'. There was a decided feeling against such a change. Mr. Andrews pointed out that there might be advantages to be secured which would make it desirable that the request, if urged by the Corporation, should be acceded to. It was arranged that if the request was formally made by the Corporation the matter should be brought before the committee again with a view to ascertaining the view of the residents in Anson Road on the subject.

Apart from this reference, there is no account in the minute books of any preliminary discussions between the Trust Committee and

---

[1] Minutes, 25th January 1902.

61

the Corporation. It may have been that the breaking of the building tie gave encouragement to those who believed that the Park was
standing in the way of progress in the shape of the extension of the
city area, and an increase in rateable value of the city property.
Certainly it came out later that there was a substantial minority in
favour of not opposing the extension. It seems clear that the city
felt that it would have support from some residents.

At the meeting of the Committee (18th September 1902) it was
proposed by Mr. Hopkinson 'that an enquiry by circular should be
made to the owners and occupiers in the Park, as to whether they
objected to trams running through Anson Road, and that when the
replies were secured, a further meeting should be held'. The Committee could not have felt entirely secure in their position for it was
also resolved that

if it became necessary in the meantime to discuss the question of any clauses
with the Town Clerk, the Honorary Secretary was directed to endeavour
to obtain clauses whereby the maintenance of the gates and the right to
charge tolls and all other existing rights were to be recognised, and that the
Corporation should provide a wood pavement along the centre of Anson
Road for running trams, and take the burden of the repair of the road in
future, and also that the rights of running trams should be restricted to
Anson Road.

The circular was prepared and published on 3rd October 1902. It
contained nothing but the bare facts of the case, with no mention
of land values or legal precedents. A small voting card was attached
so that owners and residents could vote as they wished. The date
of the counting was fixed for the 10th.

Possibly with the intention of forestalling collective action on the
part of the residents, the Corporation fixed a Town's meeting for
the 9th, 'for the purpose of consenting or otherwise, and adopting
resolutions in reference to the promotion by the City Council in the
next session of Parliament, the Manchester Corporation Bill'.

Not to be outmanœuvred, the Trust Committee rapidly prepared two circulars for Park residents, Trust Committee members,
and residents of Anson Road. The circular that was sent to the
Committee members and to Anson Road residents was couched in
slightly more alarming and dramatic terms. It stated, 'If the residents in the Park are to resist this attempt, they should take the
trouble to personally attend and vote against any resolution in
favour of it'. . . . 'If any resident receiving the circular should know
of any other in the Park who is willing to attend, it would be an
advantage to induce him to do so, as unless we have a large attendance in opposition to the scheme, the chance of resisting it later
on will be very small.' The second circular, sent to 'residents who
had objected by postcard to trams running along Anson Road', was

put out two days before the proposed Town's Meeting. It pointed out that 'any ratepayer had the right to vote whether resident in the Park or not. The Trust Committee hope you will attend and bring as many friends with you as you can to vote against the resolution. . . .'

This very vigorous Town's meeting was fully reported in the press.[1] 'The Lord Mayor presided, and there were present the Town Clerk, and a number of members of the Corporation. There was a very full attendance of burgesses.'

After an attempt by Fox, the honorary secretary of the Trust, to get alleged non-ratepayers removed, the Mayor said 'that the Manchester City Extension Act of 1885 contained certain reservations which would have to be reconsidered in view of the demand for tramways, and in the event of the passing of the resolution, they would confer with persons interested in Victoria Park'. Councillor Boyle, in seconding the resolution, pointed to the hundreds of acres in the neighbourhood of Victoria Park which were undeveloped because there were not sufficient means of access to them. This was greeted by cries of 'No!' 'What the Corporation wanted to do,' he continued, 'was to develop their tramway system within the boundaries of the city, and so to increase the rateable value. They wished also to give the citizens living within their area healthy and proper conditions.' Councillor Boyle was quite aware that Victoria Park had been a private park (A voice, 'It *is* a private park'), but it was rapidly changing its character. ('No! No!') The Corporation wanted to open up their park at Birchfields, and enable the people of Chorlton-on-Medlock to get there without the necessity of walking two-thirds of a mile.

The main defence for the Trust Committee was put by Mr. Fox, the Secretary. His grounds were that 'the extension of the tramways was not required either by the citizens, or by individuals whom it would be supposed to serve. (Applause.) There were only 26 houses in Anson Road, and the population on each side of it was very sparse.' Fox did not share Mr. Boyle's feelings about the extension of the city. In fact, he argued that 'Mr. Boyle was twenty-five years ahead of his time.' He claimed also that the effect on land values would be disastrous and that 'every house in Anson Road would change hands if this proposal were carried out, because it would be impossible for them to live in comfort with the noise and change in the locality that a line of trams would cause'. He claimed that property on the other side of the Park would not be developed because, until the Corporation did something about Black Brook, 'not a soul would come to live in the area'. He claimed that the scheme would cost the Corporation £2,000 per annum, though he did not specify how, and submitted finally, 'that the Corporation had no right to

[1] *Manchester Guardian*, 11th October 1902; *Manchester Courier*, 11th October 1902.

disturb the agreement [of 1885] especially, as in the meantime £50,000 had been spent in the Park by people who had bought land and erected houses'. Several of the aged residents spoke against the motion. Mr. Salomonson said that he had lived in the Park for fifty-seven years, 'and knew that there was strong objection to this proposal on the part of his fellow residents'. The only resident who spoke against the opposition of the Park Trust, was R. D. Darbishire,[1] a Nonconformist of considerable local standing, and a well-known local public benefactor. He had resided in the Park for twenty-five years and said that in the interests of the public the resolution should be passed. He went on, 'It is nonsense to talk about Victoria Park as a place reserved for public enjoyment. It was carefully walled round in almost every yard of its roads. The public could walk under certain trees that overshadowed the walls and footpaths, but they did not enjoy the gardens which the owners kept for their selfish and exclusive enjoyment.' Mr. Darbishire went on to challenge the very foundation of the Trust's case by claiming that 'they (meaning the Corporation and the citizens) were not bound to observe respect for its position, even though a clause was inserted in the 1885 Act, on which the opponents of the present proposal were relying to maintain the character of the Park.' He held that it was desirable that a line of tramways should be laid through the Park in the interests of the public.'

The *Manchester Guardian* described the final stages of the meeting in the following words: 'The discussion was continued amid a good deal of excitement and confusion, which increased when the Lord Mayor called upon Mr. Boyle, who speaking amid continued interruption, said he hoped that the resolution would be passed so that the tenants of Victoria Park, the representatives of the Trust, and the Corporation could settle conditions amongst themselves.' This attempt failed, however, for the motion was lost.

The immediate sequel to these events was continued controversy in the columns of the *Manchester Guardian*. During the following week Mr. Darbishire stated in full his criticism of the authority of the Trust Committee, and the evidence on which it was based. After summing up the alleged historical origins of the Trust, and stating his full awareness of clause 48 of the 1885 Act, he went on, 'For a long time I accepted the alleged authority, but recently it happened to me to investigate the whole title, in particular relating to the late Mr. Callender's house, called Ashburne House, now used by Owens College as a hostel for young lady students, and also my own house and garden adjoining.' He went on to state categorically:

I was not a little surprised to find, as a matter of fact, that the Victoria Park so-called Trust, was neither more nor less than a private arrangement of

[1] See chap. V, p. 58.

those land owners who chose to enter into it, and the so-called Trust is non-existent, and any action on its part, or on the part of any committee appointed by it, is a mere assumption, is purely voluntary, and, I must say, a singularly selfish and uncitizenlike appropriation.

He attacked the claim that the Park was 'a public resort for neighbours and children'. He continued: 'It is too ridiculous for the owners to pride themselves upon so beneficent a title when almost every one of them jealously shuts out passengers along the roads, from enjoying even a sight of anything within his purse-proud walls.' Stating his legal objections in greater detail, Darbishire laid particular stress on the fact that the original Company supported by the Act of Parliament had ceased to exist shortly after its inception, and the particular properties formally reconveyed and re-leased to the original land-owners: 'After the execution of that deed of reconveyance, the Company and its rights were literally at an end, and the lands restored free to the original land owners, from whom all recent titles are traced.'

Darbishire also contended that the levying of tolls was unauthorized, as far as the original scheme was concerned '. . . the so-called Trust, or its Committee, has for a long time charged toll at the entrance gates on vehicles, contrary to the express rights of my predecessors at least'. Rounding off, he stated: 'My words [at the public meeting] were ineffective, perhaps not heard—and the purpose of the landowners' combine asserted.' Finally, he wished 'to separate myself from even the appearance of concurrence, not only in the illiberal resolution, but in the absolutely unjustifiable pretence of aggressive and exclusive rights, and the assertion of a non-existent "Trust" '.[1]

In answer to this long and bitter reproach the secretary of the Trust, Mr. Fox, composed a short, but admirably clever reply, which combined an admission of the truth of the facts as Darbishire had presented them with a cunning re-definition of the 1902 tramway problem. He drew the distinction between 'a lawyer's question' about land titles and 'the public question, for the meeting, whether it was desirable or necessary to run trams along Anson Road'. Fox accused Darbishire of false representation, claiming that his letter conveyed the impression that the Park was governed 'through a private arrangement of the landlords', whereas in fact 'the residents as well as the owners annually elect the Victoria Park Trust Committee'.

The following two meetings of the Trust Committee cleared up the matter completely. The result of the original canvass to discover the attitude of the residents to the proposed tramways was declared at 187 against and 30 for the proposed resolution. At the same meet-

[1] *Manchester Guardian*, 15th October 1902.

ing a letter was received from Edwyn Holt[1] as to his intention to watch the interests of the Park residents in the Manchester Council in future, and it was resolved that such letter should be printed and sent with a circular to the residents.

In a celebration of their success the Committee and residents made 'a very handsome present of silver, and an illuminated address was presented to the secretary [the solicitor Fox] as a recognition of his services'.[2]

The coming of the motor car expressly challenged the wish of the Park Committee to keep the area private and noise free. Although persons had rights of passage on paying tolls, the change from horse-drawn vehicles to motor-driven cars gave opportunity, both to the Park Committee and those wishing to pass through the Park, to reassess existing agreements in the light of the definition of the new mode of transport. The Park tried to exclude the motor car, but the period ended with the courts permitting access to all on payment of toll.

On 20th July, 1905, the Park Committee received a letter from John Cooper declining to pay tolls on passing through the Park in his motor car. He based his refusal on permission he had received from Sir William Anson to free passage as a resident of the Birchfield estate. He wrote: 'I had notice from Sir William Anson's agents that his tenants had a right of way for vehicular traffic through the park. I think there must be some mistake.'

In reply to this communication Fox, on behalf of the Committee, flatly denied the relevance of the agreement with Sir William Anson to the new mode of transport, justifying his claim on the wish of the Anson Road residents, and particularly the extra wear on roads that would undoubtedly arise. He continued: 'our arrangement with Sir William Anson did not extend to motor cars, they were not then in use . . . £2.2.0d is the charge for motorists who prefer not to pay each time they wish to use these private roads . . .'[3]

Then followed a minor exercise in linguistic analysis. Cooper's solicitors wrote: 'You say that your arrangement with Sir William Anson did not extend to motor cars. It did, however, we believe, extend to vehicles, and surely a motor car is, for purposes of this kind, a vehicle. We are afraid that we must press the matter as far as residents on the Birch Estate are concerned.'

---

[1] Edwyn Holt, solicitor, Platt Lane, Rusholme. A glance at press reports of local election of this time indicates that Victoria Park hardly figured. Holt, councillor for Rusholme 1893–1904, had a high local reputation earned as chairman of the Watch Committee, in which he had vigorously forwarded the interest of sound government. In 1902 Holt defeated 'the brewery candidate' in an election in which 'public attention was directed to the Rusholme ward' (*Manchester Guardian*, 3rd November 1903). The other two councillors were G. Ashton and H. Plumner. The alderman was McDougal. None lived in Victoria Park.

[2] Minutes, 28th January 1903.   [3] Letter, 8th September, 1905.

But Mr. Fox stuck to his definition, relying on the argument that motor cars 'could not have been meant by "vehicle", since they were not yet contemplated; if motor cars, then why not any vehicle however destructive of roads or annoying to residents by reason of noise or dust. Even now, restricted by payment, the residents complain of the dust arising from motor cars which is blown into the houses.'

Although the concession had been extended to bicycles, since the agreement, Fox maintained that the Committee would not consent to the concession being further extended. Cooper's solicitors were then forced to the core of the question: 'It seems to us, that the whole question turns on whether a motor car is a vehicle—as, if it is, and personally we have no doubt on the point—it would seem to us an impossible position for your committee to take up, viz: to admit, say, a horse brougham, and refuse, say, an electric brougham . . .'[1]

On 13th October 1905 the Victoria Park Trust Committee directed the secretary to write to Sir William Anson's agents that 'they could not accede to the proposal'. Anson, however, was determined to extend this privilege, and instructed his agents to inform the committee that his intention was to put the matter to a test, if the attitude of the committee was persisted in.

Now this once more raised the question as to whether Anson, as owner of land descended in title from the owner of land outside and inside the Park, could, if he wished, remove the Anson Road gate. Fox, writing to the committee after legal advice had been sought, wrote, 'we have to face the position as to whether Anson can or cannot remove the gates in Anson Road by virtue of the covenants affecting the lands where these gates stood . . .' The most that counsel could state was that 'there should be no barrier against persons who owned the land in 1836 and their successors, but that our right to exclude the public possibly existed'. But Sir William Anson did not set up any claim that the public could have any rights. Again, therefore, as owner of the gate and of land on which the gate stood, he was able to force the committee to accede to his request. Fox wrote sardonically: 'We had better admit the motor cars. The class of house which is being built and will be built upon the estate is not likely to be occupied by gentlemen owning motor cars.'

The following day, 9th November 1905, the honorary secretary wrote to Sir William Anson's agents accepting the position 'that the motor car might fairly be considered a vehicle, and should be included in the arrangement that was made some years ago'. In any case there was 'little possibility of more than two or three motor cars being used by the residents of the Birch Hall Estate'.

[1] Letter, 15th September 1905.

F

By 1914 it seems to have been common for certain persons, particularly belonging to the medical profession, serving the growing number of nursing homes in the Park, to attempt to pass into the Park without paying tolls. The motor car would be more difficult to stop and probably more frightening. In 1914 rising prices promised to increase the Park's expenses, and so, on 22nd April 1914, 'the Honorary Secretary was instructed to inform the gatemen that greater vigilance generally was required from them, as the annual expenses would no doubt be increased'.

Now a certain Dr. R. A. Burditt of Laurel Road, Moss Side, 'had for some time been accustomed to drive his car through the Park without paying tolls. On 25th April and 2nd May the gate keeper demanded toll, and on 9th May when he saw the doctor's car approaching the Oxford Place gate, he shut this in front of him.'[1]

Burditt brought an action against the Trust Committee in the Manchester County Court, claiming fifteen guineas for damage to his motor car. The defendants claimed £1.4s.10d as damage to the toll bar, 1s.6d. for three days' toll for the use of the Park roads, and an injunction to restrain the plaintiff from using the roads except in accordance with the rules.[2]

Mr. Pearson, acting for the defendant, claimed that as Burditt was approaching the exit, the Park keeper raised his hand. When he was about twenty-two yards from it, the keeper swung the gate across his course with the result that the car came into violent contact with it. He submitted that instead of taking the law into his own hands and doing what was obviously a dangerous act, the keeper should have enforced the payment of the toll by some due process of law. The plaintiff stated that he had used the Park for some ten or eleven years and had never paid toll. However, he admitted that he would have been able to stop his car if he had realized that it was a matter of life and death, and that he had applied all his brakes, but he had not anticipated the act of the keeper. He further claimed that he had the right to use the Park roads from Sir William Anson, who had given all members of the Anson Golf Club permission.

For the defence, evidence was given by the keeper and an independent witness said that the keeper had held up his hand to warn the plaintiff when he was actually seventy-four yards away, and closed the bar when he was twenty-eight yards away. A second keeper added that on several occasions the plaintiff had disregarded his warnings to pull up, and had dashed through with the remark, 'It's all right!' Dr. Eastham, for the defence, disclaimed negligence, as the plaintiff was admittedly a trespasser, and there *could* be no negligence in closing the bar when the car was twenty-eight yards

---

[1] *Short History of Victoria Park*, p. 22.
[2] *Manchester Guardian*, 25th June 1914.

away. If the plaintiff were allowed to proceed in this way, everyone else would claim the right.

The judge doubted the evidence of the defence, for 'he could not believe that the doctor would have continued his course if he had seen the bar closed to him when he was 28 yards away'. On the other hand, 'he had every sympathy with the residents of the Park in their efforts to preserve its privacy'. He cited the clause 48 as justifying the levying of tolls, and judged that the plaintiff had acted unreasonably, and had taken a wrong view of his rights. There would be judgement for the defendants for the tolls of 1s.6d. and also an injunction restraining the plaintiff from using the roads in future except in accordance with the rules. The Committee had to pay damages for the repair of the car.

The remaining chapters describe the further encroachments on the Park by public transport, and the final opening of one of its main streets, Anson Road, to Corporation transport. Although the trams had been excluded for the time being, the rapid growth of South Manchester after 1920, and the now undeniably changing character of the area, made defence against the Corporation's demands increasingly difficult.

CHAPTER VII

THE INVASION OF TRAMWAYS, 1920, AND THE OPENING OF ANSON ROAD, 1938

After the 1914–18 war it was decided by the Manchester Corporation to develop the Anson estate, a large tract of land lying to the south of the Park. The question of transport services through the Park, along Anson Road, therefore came up. On 22nd January 1919, the Trust secretary was able to ally the fears of the Trust Committee by reporting 'that the Corporation Bill ... only referred to water charges, and that there was no clause dealing with tramways or other matters which might affect the Trust, and after a general discussion relating to the development of the Anson Estate, it was decided to leave the appointment of a sub-committee to deal with the matter of tramways. ...'

Although no further action had been taken by the Corporation, at the next meeting 'a small sub-committee of the chairman, J. H. Stubbs, the Treasurer, and the Secretary, was elected to consider what action, if any, should be adopted with reference to the extension of the Corporation tramways, and to call meetings of the whole committee when necessary'.[1] Later, the secretary forwarded a long letter to the Town Clerk on behalf of the Committee. The letter made the usual claims for the area, pointing out quite bluntly: 'Reference to maps of the Victoria Park area must unavoidably have brought the Corporation's notice to the effect that the proposed extension would have upon the future maintenance of the Park area, on its existing basis.'[2] The letter went on to affirm the Committee's intention namely, 'that these proposals leave them no alternative but to protest most strongly against this particular extension, and to intimate their intention to oppose the scheme by all lawful means'. The Committee wished to balance against the benefit of the proposed housing schemes the loss that would be incurred by those living immediately to the north of the development area. '... they must be satisfied that the objects desired, cannot be achieved without involving the very large number of inhabitants in the Park area in the sacrifice of a considerable part of the value of their property, and the loss of that seclusion which is so necessary

[1] Minutes, 19 February 1919.
[2] Letter in Bosdin Leech MSS, 18th October 1919.

for the health of persons who occupy the many homes and institutions within the area'.

On behalf of the Committee, Fox was not satisfied 'that in the best interests of the Town, this particular extension should be proceeded with ... and thought that all other aspects of the case should be considered'. The Committee must have been under the impression that time was short, and their chances of success slim, for Fox wished to raise 'the whole question of the future of the Park area, indicating the seriousness with which this plan was taken'. He went on:

As it is impossible, at a public meeting, to properly consider what I might term the overriding necessity for this extension, may I ask you to afford myself, and a small sub-committee of the Park Trust, an interview before the Town's meeting, when the question of the future of the Park area as a whole could be discussed, as this extension undoubtedly raises the larger question; and it is for the sake of the future of the whole Victoria Park area, and not from any desire to impede development of the Town's tramways or undertakings, that has induced my Committee to lodge this objection ...[1]

In reply, the Town Clerk pointed out that the coming meeting was not a town's meeting, 'but a special meeting of the City Council'.

The Park Committee met the negotiations committee, and then proceeded to interview the Parliamentary sub-committee. A memorandum prepared by Fox the Secretary stated very explicitly the Trust Committee's reasons, being 'financial, namely the loss of Park rate, which would result from Anson Road being altered to an ordinary street with trams, and the expense of collecting tolls for the use of the remaining roads'. The Victoria Park Trust Committee therefore suggested that, 'either (i) this proposal should be abandoned, or (ii) that the Victoria Park area should be dealt with as a whole, and no part of it dealt with separately'.

On the first point, Fox claimed,

   (i) that the extension had not been shown to be essential,
  (ii) that the Park was necessary as a 'non-densely occupied area' as the town expands,
 (iii) that those engaged in medical and education work residing within easy reach of the Royal Infirmary and the University, needed the area for 'rest and quietness',
 (iv) an increase in service institutions, for example schools, nursing homes, and particularly for housing University students was contemplated.

As to the second suggestion, i.e. that the Victoria Park area should be dealt with as a whole, the Trust Committee maintained that

[1] Minutes, 18th October 1919.

(a) ... at present, very few (if any) houses under the New Housing Scheme have been erected, and that in any event, this particular extension should not be commenced until at least 500 houses are erected, and the nearest tramway for which would be Birchfields Road,

(b) the Corporation should take powers to include Victoria Park within their jurisdiction and to repeal Section 48 of the 1885 Manchester Extension Act on terms equitable to the owners. Such terms should comprise the taking over the highways repairable by them, the maintenance of those roads as unpaved roads, the use of which is prohibited to street organs, hawkers, beggars, etc., ... and that heavy traffic should be prohibited, other than the particular tram traffic in Anson Road.

A Committee of five persons, 'including representatives from the medical profession and the University', were ready to discuss the matter with the Parliamentary sub-committee.[1] Before this meeting took place, some effort was made by the Trust Committee to organize the opposition, based on representation from,

(i) the frontages along Anson Road,
(ii) the interests of the Church in the Park,
(iii) the University.

A list of frontages was prepared, particularly with reference to the Park rate. Along Anson Road £70 was contributed annually to the internal rate of the area. All frontagers were, of course, opposed to the scheme. The Secretary approached the Rev. C. R. Pattison Muir[2] privately concerning the interest of the Church in the Park. The Rector replied that there were five church institutions in the area, writing,

You will gather from this that the Church of England's interests in Victoria Park are very considerable and it would be highly detrimental to the training, intellectual and physical, of the large number of students involved if the Park should lose its advantages. It seems almost unnecessary to add how greatly it must enhance the value of Manchester as an educational centre when it possesses so suitable a locality as Victoria Park.[3]

Fox also wrote about University opposition to A. Donald[4] of 5, Conyngham Road, who replied that he 'had an interview with Sir Henry Miers,[5] who said that he would be very pleased to help us, and would attend the meeting of the Parliamentary sub-committee if he possibly could. ... If he finds that he can't be present, you

[1] Minutes, 14th November 1914.
[2] Rector of St. Chrysostom's.
[3] Private letter contained in Bosdin Leech papers, dated 8th November 1920.
[4] Professor of Obstetrics and Gynaecology.
[5] Vice-Chancellor of the University.

might ask him to send someone else who would be able to state the University position strongly.'[1]

In spite of this weighty opposition, the Corporation were not to be moved. They were not adamant that the gates should be taken down, and the road thrown open to the public, but were prepared to maintain Anson Road, 'in return for the privilege of running a double track through it'.[2] At this date, however, no settlement had been reached. The Trust therefore continued with its preparations, and contacted solicitors in London who in turn contacted Parliamentary agents. Though, in fact, a settlement was reached *before* a petition was presented, the agents acted on the assumption that the controversy would continue and had petitions prepared and printed.

It is interesting to note the grounds on which the petition was prepared. In instructing Counsel, the Trust had laid great stress on the historical continuity which existed from the original company to the present Trust. In their reply on preparation, the agents (Lewis, Gregory and Anderson, S.W.1) stated,

you will see that we have not referred in the petition to the Act of 1836, and for this reason, that it appears to us that the Committee can in no sense be said to be acting in exercise of the powers of trust act, or as successors of the company which was incorporated by it and it is better to base the right of the committee to be heard against the Bill, on the ground that they have exercised control over the Park for so long a period ...

The agents made the petition, 'specifically apply to the frontagers along Anson Road, most of whom, it would appear from your instructions, contribute substantially to the Voluntary Park rate'.[3]

The crucial negotiations took place at the end of February. It appears that the Park had to be content with what they could get, for the owners of the property along Anson Road were 'sacrificed' to the rest of the area. There is no evidence that the Corporation 'threatened' to take over the whole area, in answer to the Park's alternative (which was presumably a piece of bluff). The Corporation very probably realized that the Park's future bargaining position must inevitably be weakened by the passage of trams, that those owners of property as opposed to institutions would lessen in number, and hence the primary reason for the existence of the Trust, namely, the preservation of land values, would steadily diminish.

On 25th February 1920, the Secretary reported that

there was reason to doubt (the word 'believe' is crossed out in the minute book) that a settlement on satisfactory lines would be effected; the only substantial question outstanding being the amount of the annual contribution

[1] Letter, 7th January 1920.
[2] Minutes, 20th January 1920.
[3] Letter from the agents in the Bosdin Leech papers.

to be made by the Corporation towards the upkeep of the roads adjacent to Anson Road, the residents of which would be disturbed by the proposed tramway.

On 19th February, the agents had written to the Trust Committee that the Corporation Bill had been read a second time, and five days later had written: 'if you think there is any possibility of arranging a settlement of the opposition, you should approach the Town Clerk, without prejudice, without loss of time, and ascertain what concessions (if any) the Corporation are prepared to make'.

Such agreement was reached some time between 25th February and 5th March 1920. On the 26th the agents wrote: 'we are glad to hear that there is a prospect of an amicable settlement being arrived at between the Corporation and yourselves . . .' and on 5th March, the Town Clerk wrote, 'I have received your letter . . . I have to say that, subject to what my Parliamentary Agents have to suggest, the clause, as altered by you and with the substitution of £100 for £75 is quite satisfactory to me, and I am writing to my agents accordingly.'

On 9th March 1920, Fox received word from the agents that they were in communication with the agents for the Corporation and had asked them to let the Trust Committee have an undertaking to amend the clause[1] accordingly and upon receipt of this undertaking the Petition would be withdrawn. It was withdrawn on 10th March 1920.

The Act provided under Section 33 (power to make tramways) and Section 35 (Anson Road tramways), that,

(i) the Corporation could alter the gates in Anson Road, so as to allow the construction and working of two lines of tramways, so as to afford free passage for tramway cars to the Birchfield Estate.

(ii) so long as Anson Road be used for such tram traffic by the Corporation,

   (a) the Corporation shall maintain with such material to be selected by the Corporation as will give a reasonably smooth surface, and so far as is reasonably practicable, lessen the noise in Anson Road.

   (b) Until the existing roads in Victoria Park shall become highways repairable by the inhabitants at large, and until the Victoria Park Trust ceases to exist, whichever happens first, the Corporation shall pay the sum of £100 per annum, to the Victoria Park Trust Committee, for the maintenance and repair of such existing roads, other than the said portion of Anson Road.

   (c) Anson Road shall continue as a private road, within the meaning of Section 48 of the Manchester City Extension Act, but no tolls shall be payable in respect of the use of Anson Road.

   (d) The Victoria Park Trust, shall be responsible for the maintenance of the altered gates and for such periodical closing of the same,

[1] This was the clause specifying the amount of compensation to be paid to the Park Committee.

as may be necessary for securing the privacy of Victoria Park—
but such gates shall not be closed against tramcars, or the
vehicles of the Corporation.[1]

From the evidence that remains of these negotiations, it is clear
that Manchester Corporation was granting a concession in permitting the gates of Anson Road to remain standing. Presumably,
this was all that 'influence' could manage. The fact that the
Parliamentary agents refused to word the petition on 'traditional'
grounds shows that the break with the past had come. The coming
of the trams was the final death-blow to privacy. Once the Park
had been cut in two, no conceivable arrangement of the precedents
could justify further exclusions of traffic and persons. On the other
hand, it suited the City to keep a formal privacy intact, thereby
absolving them of the responsibility for making up the roads by a
definite date. The Corporation kept the whip hand by being able
to 'threaten' a complete takeover thus involving inhabitants in
heavy road charges, but avoided such a course by permitting a
nominal privacy so long as some gates remained standing.

The changes inside and outside the Park which reflected the
growing urbanization of Manchester led in the 1930s to specific
administrative problems, particularly to the then new difficulty of
city traffic congestion. The following tables indicate how numbers of
vehicles on the roads had increased since 1920 and roughly how
much traffic was passing along certain streets.

TABLE ONE*

LICENCES FOR VEHICLES ISSUED IN MANCHESTER

Vehicle	1921	1938
Private motor cars	3951	28759
Motor cycles	3926	5998
Goods vehicles	3216	9689
Hackneys	800	1249

* Tables contained in Chief Constable's Report, 1938

TABLE TWO*

LICENCES ISSUED

	1921	1938
Driving Licences issued in Manchester	16848	50912

[1] Copy of the 1920 agreement contained in the Bosdin Leech papers.

TABLE THREE*

VEHICLES PASSING ALONG CERTAIN STREETS

Street	Number
Stockport Road	14310
Brook Street—Upper Brook Street	14126
Oxford Road—Wilmslow Road	12307
Oldham Road	11208
Cheetham Hill Road	10928
Princess Road—Parkway	10173

* Tables contained in Chief Constable's *Report*, 1938. Table Three accompanied by the following, 'The traffic volumes quoted in this table are averages based on available statistics and should be used merely as an indication and not as exact figures.'

Two very important facts emerge from these tables:
  (i) that the roads of which Anson Road is an extension, namely Upper Brook Street, had become second in a list of fifteen arterial roads leading out of the city,
  (ii) that this road lies between the two roads which pass along the extremities of the Park, and which are the first and third on the list. The Upper Brook Street outlet was also third on the list of ratings of accidents per one tenth of a mile. These facts amply demonstrate the importance of Anson Road as an outlet to the south of the city

On 24th March 1938, a special meeting of the executive committee of the Trust Committee was called, 'for the purpose of discussing the suggestion which had appeared in the newspapers, that the Manchester Corporation should free Anson Road from tolls'. At the previous meeting (21st January 1938) the Chairman, Mr. Bell, had stated, 'that the Traffic Congestion Committee, of which he was a member, had instructed the Town Clerk to enquire into the position of Anson Road and the Park tolls'.

1935–1937

TOLL COLLECTIONS AT THE 6 GATES

	Anson Road	Oxford Place	Long-sight	Upper Brook Street	Rusholme	Victoria Road	Total
1935	£169	67	101	301	65	51	754
1936	187	64	97	328	67	49	792
1937	188	67	93	322	68	51	789

Contracts £286, £311, and £305 respectively, which should be added to the two main gates, bringing the totals to £1050, £1103 and £1094 respectively. So far 1938 is up on 1937.

Wages were £665 in 1937 and other years about the same. This figure is for the six gates; the wages at the two gates in Anson Road amount to approximately £300.

Councillor Jackson, who later became chairman of this increasingly anachronistic body, intimated that he had discussed the matter with the Town Clerk, and had suggested that, rather than that the Corporation should seek to force the position in any way, the matter might be discussed amicably between the Corporation representatives of the Park Trust, in order to see whether some friendly arrangement could be arrived at. He stated that the principal reason behind the Corporation's wishes was the concern of the Chief Constable over traffic congestion.

It is quite clear from the discussion that followed that Councillor Jackson was very much the representative of the Corporation, rather than the champion of the Park. The position of the Council was unassailable. It was therefore imperative for the Park to obtain the best terms they could for the opening of Anson Road. This Jackson seems to have done, without involving the Corporation in extensive road commitments.

Dr. Bosdin Leech, probably the keenest Park lover and champion of the full take-over scheme, suggested that the Committee might ask that, in consideration of Anson Road being thrown open, the remaining toll gates should be dispensed with, and that the Corporation should agree over a term of years, not to insist on the full normal standard of road making in the Park, but that they should agree to maintain the roads in no worse condition than they were at that moment, and to the satisfaction of the Park Committee.

Councillor Jackson put forward what must have been the Corporation's view that the existing toll gates, apart from those in Anson Road, might be maintained, and another toll gate should be erected in order not to maintain the Park in two separate districts either side of Anson Road, in the same way that the Park is maintained at present. It was clear to the Committee that this must be the scheme that would be proposed by the Corporation officially, for the income from the Anson Road gate was considered to be relevant. An analysis of these figures was to be prepared and sent to the Corporation as soon as possible.

Before the meeting with the Corporation Dr. Bosdin Leech, obviously feeling very strongly the weakness of the Park's position, wrote to the chairman in an attempt to persuade him that his analysis of the position was the true one. He wrote on 29th March, 1938, that he felt that the Executive Committee had misunderstood his views at the meeting of the 24th, and felt constrained to make the following points:

(i) We may oppose the opening of Anson Road altogether.

(ii) We may agree to the opening of Anson Road in return for some valuable consideration, and continue to govern the park.

(iii) We may realise that (ii) would be unworkable if Anson Road were thrown open to the public, and should bargain for the Park as a whole to be taken over by the town on favourable terms.

Dr. Bosdin Leech went on to say that he thought that any terms that the town might offer would be unacceptable. 'When once Anson Road is thrown open to the public, the Park would not hold together, and it would rapidly deteriorate till the town, having the upper hand, would force the inhabitants to pave the roads at their own expense.'

He suggested that after a reasonable fight for scheme (i), they should try to bargain for scheme (ii) and ask for the best possible terms, viz.,

(a) that the town should take over all paving costs,
(b) that the roads should be kept in a condition no worse than at present,
(c) that the Park should be treated as a special area in view of
   (i) the large number of institutions in it,
   (ii) the advantage that the open space has been and still is to the community,
   (iii) the fact that full local rates have been paid for 100 years without cost for road making,
(d) that the Park Committee should exist, and be recognised for a limited time to protect the interests of the inhabitants.

These ambitious suggestions had however no effect, for it was reported at the next meeting of the Trust Committee 'that efforts had been made to obtain some arrangement or undertaking from the Corporation regarding the paving of the Park roads, but had not been successful'. The issue of the eventual cost of paving, had it to be borne by the residents, was holding the Park together, for 'in the event of the Corporation forcing paving, the representatives of certain institutions intimated that they might find it necessary to withhold their payment of the Park rate, to accumulate the amount so retained annually in a fund, to meet the eventual cost of paving'. But in answer to this, the Chairman pointed out that the Committee would not be able to maintain the roads, with the eventual result that the roads would be taken over, and that paving notices would be served.

The offer of the Corporation to pay £700 was generous in the light of the fact that it was only slightly less than the income from all the gates. Mr. Kay, however, suggested that the amount offered by the Corporation would be sufficient 'but that to maintain the additional gates, the employment of one or two additional men would be necessary and for this reason he suggested that the Corporation be asked to increase their offer by £100'. The Corporation made no difficulty out of his proposal, also agreeing to pay the income tax on the £800.

The agreement was signed 30th October 1938 and laid down in particular:

The trust, so far as they lawfully do so, as the authority having control over the roads in Victoria Park, merely grant to the public . . . full right of way . . . without payment of tolls . . . on Anson Road (Clause 1)

The Corporation will pay to the Trust, in substitution for the income from tolls at present receivable from users of Anson Road, an amount computed at £800 (Clause 2)

The Corporation will pay the wages of eight of the men, who from time to time shall be employed by the Trust for collecting tolls or repairing roads (Clause 3)

The payments made under this agreement shall be in addition to the £100 payable by the Corporation under the 1920 agreement. (Clause 4)

The remaining clauses were concerned with the obligation of the Corporation to erect new toll gates along Anson Road at the junction of Oxford Place, Conyngham Road and Daisy Bank Road with Anson Road.

CHAPTER VIII

THE WAR YEARS, AND THE FINAL ABSORPTION BY MANCHESTER CORPORATION

Although the damage had been done, the surprising fact is that the Park continued so long as a private area. The second world war, though directly causing the rising costs, which later made the Park's finances completely unpracticable, permitted the shelving of the question which would ordinarily have arisen in the late 1930s, namely, the terms under which the area would have been included in the town plan. On 26th September 1939, the Secretary of the Trust Committee reported that 'he had written to the Town Clerk requesting his assurance that the Town Planning Scheme should be applied to the Park area; that the latter should be scheduled as a residential area, with the power to allow nursing homes, private hotels, residential flats, but that business premises should be prohibited'.[1] The Town Clerk had replied that he 'would communicate with the Secretary when the Town Planning Committee had completed their deliberations'.[2]

As was to be expected, the issue was not decided at this time, for at the meeting of the Trust Committee, 20th January 1940, 'no progress had been made with the Town Planning Committee regarding certain assurances asked for by the Trust in connection with the Town Planning Scheme. The chairman explained that the matter had been more or less shelved owing to the war, and consequently it was agreed to leave the matter in abeyance.' The international conflict was no respecter of what was left of the Park's privacy, and though the Committee did its best, for the most part, the area within the gates was treated in much the same way as the area without. The military moved in. A barrage balloon site appeared in the open space to the west of Conyngham Road, the American authorities took ever the Methodist College, near 'Sunbury', as a hostel, and British officers were stationed at 'High Elms'. The secretary approached both authorities, but it was reported that 'it had not been possible to arrange for any payments to be made, either by the British or the American military authorities, in respect of the use of the Park roads by their vehicles'.[3] Oddly, the Park was able to extract *some* money from the military, for 'the chair-

---

[1] Trust Committee Minutes.　　　　[2] Trust Committee Minutes.
[3] Minutes, 8th February 1944.

man reported that the authority responsible for the barrage balloon had agreed to make a contribution of £10 p.a. to the Trust'.[1]

The Committee considered itself in a special position as far as the collection of metal salvage was concerned. The official policy was that all metal railings placed round private property should be taken away for the war effort.

Mr. Kay (Hon. Sec.) reported that he had been approached by the Ministry of Works regarding the surrender of the Park gates under the metal salvage regulations. He had interviewed the department concerned, and in addition had written to them formally, setting out the difficulties with which the Park Trust would be faced, in the event of the gates being removed, particularly in the collection of tolls. He had also made certain suggestions for a compromise, by way of giving part of the gates only . . .[2]

The Ministry had agreed to await the results of the Committee's deliberations and on 8th February 1944, 'Mr. Kay reported that he had received no further communication from the authorities regarding the surrender of the railings.'[3]

The old area of the Park did not require the building of air raid shelters, but the newer property, in the east, qualified. There was opposition to the official policy, for '. . . it was reported that the authorities had wished to erect a shelter in Kedleston Road, but that the residents had petitioned against it, and it had not been proceeded with.'[4] Similar remarks applied to Victoria Road, but it appeared that one would be built in Langdale Road. However, the Chairman, Alderman Jackson, was later able to state, 'that he did not think there were likely to be any further air raid shelters erected in the Park'.[5]

Perhaps the two ways in which the ebbing life of the Park was affected by the war were the labour shortage and increased apathy. The finances of the committee, which will be examined more fully later, show that for the years 1942–44 labour costs were the lowest ever during the period 1938–52. This, coupled with the increased savings engendered by the war, enabled the Trust to ride the additional expenses of road and sewage maintenance in Daisy Bank Road. The labour shortage must have made itself felt in the general appearance of the area, for during the early years of the war there were several attempts to promote tidiness.[6] These efforts, however, could not have been very successful. Towards the end of the war complaints were appearing frequently. For example, '. . . a suggestion was put before the Committee that arrangements be made for employers of the Park to patrol in the evenings, and on Saturdays and Sundays, with a view to keeping down the mischief,

[1] Minutes, 24th January 1942.   [2] Minutes, 1st February 1943.
[3] Minutes, 8th February 1944.   [4] Minutes, 29th September 1942.
[5] Minutes, 1st February 1943.
[6] Minutes, 8th February and 23rd May 1940.

VICTORIA PARK—ANALYSIS OF ATTENDANCE AT MEETINGS, 1940–1954

1. NUMBERS PRESENT AT A.G.M.* COMPARED WITH NUMBER ON EXECUTIVE COMMITTEE

Date	1940	1941	1942	1943	1944	1945	1946	1947	1948	1949	1950	1951	1952	1953	1954
No. on Committee	25	23	23	25	20	24	24	23	23	23	25	25	25	25	25
No. present at A.G.M.	14	19	—	—	—	26	16	22	16	24	11, 40	11, 20	29	38	450

2. NUMBERS PRESENT AT QUARTERLY MEETINGS OF TRUST COMMITTEE AND NUMBERS OF APOLOGIES

Year	1940	1941	1942	1943	1944	1945	1946	1947	1948	1949	1950	1951	1952	1953
Present at quarterly meetings	6, 8, 12, 6	9, 9, 13,† 6, 9	11, 11, 7	6, 8, 10	9, 8, 11	8†, 11, 15	11†, 13, 11	10, 9, 8	7	7, 8	7, 11†, 15	8, 12†, 15	9, 9	13†
No. of apologies read out	2, 4, 6, 4	1, 5, 3, 1, 6	6, 0, 4	2, 4, 3	3, 6, 3	3, 2, 5	3, 0, 2	3, 0, 5	1	1, 3	3, 3, 3	6, 2, 0	2, 5	7

* A.G.M. All owners and occupiers of property entitled to attend.
† More than half of Committee members present.

caused by the children throwing stones . . .'[1] At the same meeting the effect of the labour shortage on the condition of the roads was illustrated when, 'Mr. Kay had had occasion to reprimand one of the road men for not attending properly to his duties, and that the man had been doing private work for residents during the time he should have been on duty . . .' That the standards of privacy were rapidly falling into decay can be illustrated by the following, '. . . the secretary was requested to write to the superintendent of police, asking for additional police patrols in the Park area, on account of the excessive damage being done to Park Property'. At the same meeting 'Mr. Walters commented that hawking was becoming prevalent in the Park, and Mr. Kay was requested to keep a look out for such offenders'.[2]

The charge of apathy during these years is not difficult to substantiate. The tables given show that the number of Park residents who turned up at annual general meetings was only a very small fraction of those who were entitled to be present as owners and/or occupiers. It was only during the very last years of the Trust that the figure was greater than the size of the Trust Committee elected annually by the annual general meeting. Similarly, of those present at the A.G.M.s it was always the case that most were the Trust Committee members, though it was *never* the case that *all* Trust Committee members attended an A.G.M. The second table gives an analysis of the inter-A.G.M. meetings, usually held quarterly, though sometimes bi-annually. Here, the apathy is even more marked. When this table is compared with the size of the Committee, as shown in table 1, the scope of the indifference is fully visible. Out of forty-one inter-A.G.M. meetings, on only seven occasions were more than half of the Committee present. A guide to the interest shown may also be revealed by the number of members who felt obliged to inform the meetings of their intended absence through apology. On most occasions, the number of apologies received was well below half the number who were actually absent.

This then is a clear example of an organization dying from the apathy of the vast majority of its potential membership, but kept alive by the interest and the attention of a few devoted servants, working through the arrangements and institutions that really belonged to a former period. Alderman Jackson, J.P., remained chairman during the whole of the period. Mr. Max Kay was treasurer for the last eight years of his life, only resigning in 1948 on health grounds. On his retirement, Mr. S. B. Brittain became treasurer, and later in the year he was appointed to the combined position of Honorary Secretary, Treasurer and General Executive Officer, a

---

[1] Minutes, 8th February 1944.   [2] Minutes, 24th September 1945.

position he held until the end in 1954. It is clear that most of the work for the final settlement with the Corporation fell on his shoulders. On 17th September 1943, as a Committee member, he had suggested 'that the secretary be requested to prepare and submit to the next meeting a list of the attendances of the various members during the past three years'.[1] This list had disappeared, but at the time it 'was read to the meeting', and as a result 'some of the larger institutions in the Park area, whose members had not attended regularly, were asked to send representatives to our meetings in view of the fact that such institutions were vitally concerned in the matters of policy affecting the Park area'. In 1944 apparently for the first time, representatives from the Church of St. Chrysostom's, the Christain Science Church, St. Joseph's Convent and the Xaverian College were invited to attend the meetings of the Committee. Other institutions which were represented were the Unitarian College, the Rusholme Conservative Club, St. Mary's, Hulme Hall and St. Anselm's.

The final indication of apathy may be seen in the complete breakdown of the election procedure. Democratic procedure must have been badly strained, with an A.G.M. electing a committee of twice its own size, but in 1949, and thereafter, the minute book shows the election *en bloc* of the Trust Committee, and after 1950, of the chief officers. After 1953 'all officers continued as at present until the termination of the Trust'.

The general financial decline of the Park and the arrangements that were made with the Manchester Corporation in the years prior to 1954 for the taking over of the area by that body will now be reviewed. On 25th January 1941 Mr. Kay reported that 'in response to complaints from residents in Daisy Bank Road, the roadmen had endeavoured to trace the stoppage in the sewers in that road, that they had not been successful, and he had had to call in the Corporation.' It transpired that the matter could only be put right by the laying of a new sewer, the cost of which and of the labour already incurred would be considerable, probably well over £100. Dr. Bosdin Leech raised the question as to whether the Park Trust was liable for this considerable expense, and it was eventually agreed that Mr. Kay should consult a solicitor. The outcome of these consultations was that the Committee could not call upon the Corporation to pay the charges in question. It was agreed therefore that the Committee had no option but to accept the position. Alderman Jackson stated that he would interview the Corporation department concerned with a view to having the work carried out at the minimum cost.[2]

As it turned out, the Corporation had grossly underestimated the cost of the necessary repairs and additions: 'The chairman explained

[1] Minutes.	[2] Minutes, 8th February 1941.

that the charges were so heavy that before accepting the account he felt it advisable to consult his colleagues.'[1] Alderman Jackson had already asked Mr. Tweedale to send a letter to the Town Clerk asking for a small deputation to be allowed to meet some of the members of the Public Health Committee to discuss the whole situation. The grounds for the Trust's opposition seem to have been two-fold, for 'Mr. Bell quoted certain items from the Public Health Act of 1875 which might be construed in favour of the Trust as coming under the heading of responsibility by the authority which took over the existing sewers'. Secondly, 'it was resolved to ask the secretary to ascertain from the Town Clerk why the Corporation were dealing differently with the Trust sewers to their own'. The Trust also required to know 'under what act the account had been sent to the Trust'. At this point the Committee also decided that if a satisfactory reply was not forthcoming, to refer the matter to a K.C.

The outcome of negotiations with the Corporation was that the latter were entirely able to defend their position, and the Park was forced to pay almost to the letter the account demanded by the Corporation.[2] On behalf of the Trust, a deputation had attended upon the Town Hall officials who had the matter in hand, but the Secretary had been informed that no reduction in the amount could be made, except that the Corporation would agree to forgo the 5% establishment charge. The total bill was £588.3.3d. which was to be paid back over five years.

Mr. Kay prepared a circular which described the situation to the residents:

As the Trust is not a trading concern, and hardly manages to pay its way . . . especially with a falling income during the period of the war, this sudden and unexpected outlay is beyond its present means. Would it be too much to ask all the householders and owners of property in the Park area to make a token gift towards the extraordinary expenses? There are over 700 houses in the area, and if a sum of say, 10s.0d to £1 per house were contributed it would considerably relieve the situation.

The number of replies received was 86, and the amount raised was £72.

The end of the Trust Committee was, of course, closely tied with the Park's inability to pay its way from its main sources of income, tolls and Park rate, against the post-war mounting costs, and difficulty of obtaining labour, and particularly the cost of road repairs. The rate continued to be voluntary, and to be assessed on the general rate. That is at 1s. in the pound, on the general assessment with a limit of £20, but owners and residents who would otherwise pay £5 and upwards in respect of the Park rate were asked to con-

VICTORIA PARK TRUST—CHIEF ITEMS OF INCOME AND EXPENDITURE,* 1938–1952

Income in £	1938	1939	1940	1941	1942	1943	1944	1945	1946	1947	1948	1949	1950	1951	1952
Tolls	1020	526	452	406	399	393	365	355	417	428	446	423	441	424	409
Voluntary rate	486	450	421	395	393	374	381	391	409	447	479	546	526	677	689
Cash in Hand	30	12	20	17	11	9	28	8	10	6	111	0	1	1	1
Cash in Bank	125	220	467	634	576	708	642	833	1070	832	383	303	185	57	314
Expenditure															
Wages†	116	379	436	448	382	206	355	314	641	659	757	708	739	732	805
Roads, etc. A/c	66	145	38	33	35	47	18	35	167	118	57	71	120	64	131
Insurances		98	56	55	53	49	50	47	66	84	104	120	106	104	112
Payment on new sewers	—	—	—	142	90	290	40	—	—	—	—	—	—	—	—
Clothing, Coke and Sundries	168	137	145	142	147	137	137	147	146	167	176	174	181	77	79

* † Based on Annual Accounts contained in Minute Books, and to the nearest, £.
After deduction of £800 contribution by Manchester Corporation (as per Annual account).

tribute at the rate of 1s.3d in the £1. Actually, there could have been no compulsion on residents and occupiers to pay those rates, and contribution was very much a voluntary affair, depending on personal relations and contacts. Mr. Brittain complained, for example, that St. Joseph's 'never contributed a penny', whereas 'Brother Martin of Xaverian was always ready with £10'. It is quite certain that the vast majority of residents in the eastern half of the Park must have ignored the appeals of the Committee, and it seems likely that most of the contributions came from the institutions of the western end. From the table it can be seen that there was a steady decline in Park receipts from 1938 to 1943, from which time there was a steady increase.

Tolls naturally suffered very badly from the war. The military for the most part refused payment, and the blackout and petrol shortage must have cut private traffic tremendously. There was an immediate fall in 1939 of £500, the decline continuing to 1945. Again, after 1950, receipts from tolls declined steadily. On the expenditure side of course, the greatest blow was the general increase in costs. Wages fell off during the war, owing to the laying off of some workpeople, but in 1946 the bill immediately doubled, remained steady for a number of years, and then increased to over £800 in 1952.

These figures show only income and expenditure, and say nothing about the actual state of the roads of the Park. It is certain that as much as could be afforded was being spent, but this was a rapidly diminishing percentage of what was actually required for proper maintenance. By late 1948 it was necessary for Mr. Brittain to call a special meeting 'to hear a report as regards Park rate, and to confirm his draft circular for issue. Mr. Brittain explained we could not hope to carry out the necessary road repairs unless there was a substantial increase in Park rate, and read his circular.' This circular contained the usual exhortations to Park dwellers but also a curious veiled threat that might, had it been followed up, have led to a most anomalous position. It was pointed out particularly to the owners of cars

'that mere residence in the Park does not entitle the owner to drive his car over the roads of the area, other than his own frontage. Tolls have never been charged to residents or to friends visiting them, but the Committee will have to examine this matter where the owner does not contribute. Under Act of Parliament the Trust have power to keep all vehicles off the roads.'

This threat to charge tolls to residents had no effect. Mr. Brittain reported to the next meeting 'the result of the circular was negligible and not worth the time and trouble taken'.[1]

[1] Minutes, 3rd March 1949.

At the next A.G.M., attended by most of the Committee 'and about 40 owners and/or residents', the seriousness of the Park's position was fully stated.

'The Chairman proceeded to stress the need for more Park rate, there were still many non-subscribers, and stated that unless there was an improvement, necessary work could not be undertaken, and we should have to consider the Corporation taking over the area, which would involve all land and property owners in considerable expense for drainage and paving.'

A suggestion (not in the form of a motion apparently) was made that all owners be circulated to state:

(a) whether the Trust continue
(b) whether the local authority should take over if the income was not increased.

Later the situation was revealed as precarious, for 'The Treasurer reported an expenditure of £125 p.a. over income, and unless income was increased by this sum, the Trust could not function beyond December 1952.'

At the A.G.M. for 1951 only '20 owners and/or ratepayers' in addition to most of the Committee members turned up. Once more the Treasurer reported the precarious position, and after a discussion, 'Mr. Sampson proposed that in view of the remarks and our inability to put roads in order, all we could do was to patch up, and also, that the old-fashioned drainage could not be improved, that the Trust be wound up, and the Local Authority be asked to take over.' The Chairman accepted the resolution, but pointed out that the Committee could not accept such a grave step without further consultation, and a much larger attendance of owners who were entitled to a voice in this matter. It was decided to hold a referendum on this matter.

The referendum had incorporated an opportunity for voters to express their willingness to contribute to the voluntary rate, or to increase their contribution. Seven hundred and two papers were issued, and 399 votes were cast, 333 voted in favour of the continuation of the Trust and 66 against, 232 promised to increase their subscription.[1]

As a result of this referendum there was a slight improvement in the financial position of the Trust. For example, 'Expressions of satisfaction [by the Committee] regarding contractors' work in filling in large pot holes in the main roads were voiced. The Secretary stated the cost at £99 and such expenditure had only been possible by increased rate contribution which he hoped would continue.'[2]

This improvement, however, was short lived, for the Trust soon found itself in further difficulties. Early in 1953,

---

[1] Minutes, 18th July 1951.   [2] Minutes, 7th March 1952.

The Chairman raised the question of the state of the roads, and asked the Committee to consider whether we could really carry on much longer on the present lines . . . the appeal for increased rate had not met with the response that we had hoped for . . . the Trust could no longer repair the roads on present income . . . labour difficulties were becoming impossible.[1]

At this point, the Secretary indicated that he thought that the Corporation had already made over £500,000 profit out of the Park, in the way of lack of road repairs, and that the Park dwellers should no longer be bound by an act signed by Trust officials over fifty years ago, who at that time could not have foreseen mechanical transport.[2]

At the following A.G.M. 'after a lengthy discussion it was resolved that the time had arrived when the Trust should come to the best possible terms with the Local Authority, and that the Trust should be wound up at the earliest possible date.'[3]

Mr. Brittain lost no time in writing to the Town Clerk, Mr. Dingle, pointing out the decision taken by the Committee. Some attempt was made to oblige the Corporation to repair the surfaces, for 'the feeling of the meeting was that temporary road repair work could be undertaken by the Corporation in view of the fact that although *full* Manchester rates had always been paid, we never had any highway services, and that when the Trust is wound up, the Corporation will save the sum of £800 per year'.

Mr. Dingle replied stating the need for information about the history, constitution, and powers of the Trust, but went on to state that

probably the views of the Corporation would be based on the following assumptions:—

(a) That the roads in Victoria Park are public highways not repairable by the inhabitants at large, and

(b) that the Corporation's powers under the general law to require roads in the city to be levelled, sewered, paved, etc., at the expense of the frontages apply to roads in Victoria Park, as they apply to roads in the city outside Victoria Park.[4]

Mr. Brittain replied agreeing to the assumption that the highways were public—but only when the Trust was wound up.[5] However, it was reported to the Committee that a meeting had taken place at the Town Clerk's office on 30th September 1953,

'when it was agreed that a proposal to repeal the Victoria Park Trust Act/s and local acts relating to Victoria Park, and to provide that the roads in Victoria Park shall be deemed to be private streets, and the adjoining

[1] Minutes, 30th January 1953.   [2] Minutes, 30th January 1953.
[3] Minutes, 6th January 1953.
[4] Letter in Victoria Park records with Mr. Brittain.
[5] 6th May 1953. Letter contained in private papers of Mr. Brittain.

owners liable to pay private streets' works expenses, and these words be inserted in the Manchester Corporation Bill to be presented to Parliament in November.'[1]

Now since the Park Committee had expressed its willingness to be taken over by the Corporation it was a simple matter to draft these terms and place them in the Corporation Bill, and to wind up the Trust Committee at a meeting of land owners. The General and Parliamentary Committee reported the Manchester Corporation Bill and the sections dealing with the Victoria Park,[2] and a copy of the terms was received by Mr. Brittain on 6th March 1954. The agreement contained in Appendix One was final, except that the additional provision mentioned in clause 5 was included formally. The Corporation, of course, ceased payments in respect of Anson Road, property owners were liable for paving but not for sewers, and the Corporation took over the responsibility of the Trust as far as employees and property concerning the work of the Trust was concerned.

The Town Clerk also suggested the resolution that was to be put to the assembled meeting of the owners and occupiers of the Park, which was read, 'that this meeting approves the arrangements submitted by the Manchester Corporation relative to the paving of the unmade roads in Victoria Park, and also the inclusion in the Manchester Corporation Bill now before Parliament which would enable effect to be given thereto'.

The last circular to the Park residents was sent out containing the resolution suggested by the Corporation, and notices advertising this last meeting appeared in the *Evening News* and the *Manchester Guardian* on 26th March 1954. The last entry in the Minute Book reports this meeting, held at the College of Housecraft, High Street, at which some 450 residents and owners were present. The entry is brief, mentioning that, 'various questions were put' mostly relating to projected costs of paving and sewering. The motion was carried with one dissenter. The Park officially ceased to be private on 30th April 1954. All documents passed to the Corporation, the huts were closed, and the gates thrown open on 31st March 1954. The balance of £33.2.3d with the final account was forwarded to the Corporation on 4th June 1954.

[1] Minutes, 31st October 1953.
[2] Appendix to Council Proceedings, 1953–54, Vol. 2, pp. 1418–20.

EPILOGUE

The Park changed little as a result of formal absorption in Manchester. The process of the conversion of buildings to many different uses, which had already reached an advanced stage by 1940, continued. The most recent type of development reflects this in that one finds pairs of semi-detached houses, blocks of flats and extensions to University Halls of Residence put up in what were formerly the grounds of larger houses. Some of the older type houses were converted into flats, for example 'Holly Bank' in Oxford Place, houses in Buckingham Crescent, Addison House and the whole of Addison Terrace.

The University controls several properties. Hulme Hall comprises the buildings marked Fielden School, Oxford Lodge and Park House. St. Gabriel's consists of The Lodge, Woodthorpe and Brislington Villas on Oxford Road. Langdale Hall plus two extensions in its grounds, Dalton Hall, St. Anselm's which includes two houses opposite, and 'Eaglesfield' behind which the new Graham block (1961) of Dalton Hall has been built, all belong to the University. 'Denison House', 'High Elms' and 'Sunnyside' are nursing homes. The Roman Catholic Church is a large holder of the property in the area. The Xaverian College comprises 'Firwood' and 'Sunbury' with extensions. 'Regent House' and 'Clarence Lodge' house students training for the priesthood and 'Saville House' is a prep-school. More school building has taken place on the site of 'Redclyffe'. There is a secondary school at the junction of Denison Road and Conyngham Road.

Along Daisy Bank Road, 'Newbury' is an old people's home, 'The Limes' is a Christian Women's Hostel. 'Hirstwood' is a Methodist Young Men's Hostel and 'Summerville' is still The Unitarian College. There are several private hotels in the area, for example at 'Sapphire Villa'. 'Milverton Lodge' is a night club, taking in 'The Gables' next door. 'Gartness' has been a Toc H hostel for many years. Some houses are occupied by offices, for example, in Park Crescent 'Aulgirth', and 'Brook House' in Oxford Place.

The picture which emerges is that, after formal absorption by the Corporation of Manchester, development took place piecemeal and in an unco-ordinated way, the particular uses to which buildings were put and whether they were preserved and in what condition being very much a matter of accident. Consequently, superimposed on the unique architectural and historical unity were the chaotic results of twentieth-century urbanization.

This situation has changed somewhat with the growing interest in the environment. This expressed itself locally through the activities of the Rusholme and Fallowfield Civic Society, who began to campaign in 1971 for the preservation of some of the Park.

Meanwhile, the City Council has been considering, under the Civic Amenities Act, 1967, various proposals for Conservation Areas in the city, and ten, including the Victoria Park area, have been so declared (1976).

In addition to the statutory controls which are available to a local planning authority, the Planning Committee have adopted a fairly strict control policy. In general, buildings of some architectural merit or historic interest are retained wherever possible in preference to complete re-development, but where the latter is necessary, the new development must conform to certain criteria; low density development only is permitted, the height of buildings respecting the existing tree line. The concept of large buildings set within a lavish landscaped setting should be adhered to and existing trees on site should be retained where practicable. In a number of cases, the density of development is largely determined by the existing tree cover on site. The design of new buildings must be complementary to existing development in Victoria Park, and no flat-roofed buildings are allowed. Materials used in new construction should blend with existing materials, particularly where brickwork is concerned.

To ensure that existing trees are retained, the City Council is considering the promotion of a number of Tree Preservation Orders on key sites within Victoria Park. One Order has been confirmed to date for sites in Upper Park Road (May 1972).

The first three listed buildings within the Conservation Area, are all situated to the east of Anson Road. These are the First Church of Christ Scientist (Grade II*), Addison Terrace, Nos. 84 to 106, Daisy Bank Road (Grade II) and Milverton Lodge (Grade II). Many of the older buildings in the Park have been suggested for statutory listing by the Rusholme and Fallowfield Civic Society and the Civic Trust for the North West, and the Secretary of State for the Environment has recently (February 1976) listed nineteen further buildings and groups of buildings in the Park.

* Probably the most important, architecturally, of the buildings in the Park, designed by Edgar Wood in 1903 (J. H. G. Archer, 'Edgar Wood: a noted Manchester architect', *Trans. Lancs. & Ches. Antiquarian Society*, vols. 73-4, 1966, pp. 173-4).

APPENDIX 1

(From Sir Neville Cardus, *Second Innings*, 1950, pp. 7–11: a nostalgic, romantic view of the Park.)

There was a sequestered purlieu called Victoria Park not more than a half an hour's drive in a carriage from Manchester; the city in those years of the early nineteen-hundreds came to a sudden end on its southern side at the church in Rusholme, near the lane running along the Platt estate, a gracious pleasance with the meadows of Chorlton in the western distance and the village of Fallowfield hidden behind a clump of trees. There were toll-gates at the roads, which gave entrance to Victoria Park; no vehicle not possessed by dwellers within these select groves was admitted free of charge. Pedestrians enjoyed right of way, but, such was the sense of propriety cultivated by the lower orders of the period, none abused the privilege. Victoria Park was the preserve of wealthy German Jews; and the names of most of them were graven on burnished brass at the entrances of counting-houses of Portland Street—Schill Seebohm, Mandelberg, Maurice Spiegelberg, Hertz, Hirschberg. After a Hallé concert conducted by Hans Richter, carriages would make a procession along Oxford Road, every Thursday night, under the damp dripping arch of the railway, up the brow and past All Saints, where a churchyard was denied privacy, though none was perhaps needed now; for time and weather had rendered most of the graves and shattered pillars nameless, without dates or means of identification. Passing slums on the right, and on the left a frontage of shops feebly emulative of Oxford Street in London, including a Frascati's Restaurant, the cavalcade would go its unheeding way until High Street was reached; here was a change of air, a middle-class gentility of stucco, a bridge-passage to the Park itself.

'Carriages at 10' announced the programme of the Hallé Concerts; and they were drawn by good bloodstock, urged on and instructed in the German language. If a 'four-wheeler' should be obliged to move in the same direction, plying a habitual and utilitarian trade, the cabby knowing his place would as quickly as possible extricate himself and his hack and get close to the kerb. The ordinary denizen of Manchester, clerk or artisan, or manager of a bank at £500 a year, remembered, if ever he chanced to forget, that this was Hallé Concert night. Not all of the population of this opulent centre of industry and merchandise in the North of England could have told you exactly what went on every week at a Hallé Concert, except that it was 'classical' music, mostly German. This was

93

the age in which music was definitely not for the masses; we knew our 'Messiah' in Manchester well enough, but the names of Wagner and Tchaikovsky were exclusive and foreign and tentatively pronounced.

Inside Victoria Park, the carriages swung by iron gates and pillars, and curved along drives to massive turreted stone houses, at the base of them broad steps leading up to the portals, flanked by lions *couchant*. There was a brief opening and clapping-to of doors, a clicking of handles, a glimpse into severely upholstered interiors, then the carriage wheels crunched on the gravel again for a while, and soon the thoroughfares of the Park were vacant in the winter blackness; and none but the policeman witnessed the lights go out after midnight, first in the wide casements looking on the lawns, a little later in the bedrooms above.

I hold a memory of a dining-room in one of these houses, heavy furniture and a *Stammbaum* on the wall, a family tree branching like a Banyan, dates and names down the ages from Hanover. On the wall above the sideboard, where a bowl of oranges glowed in the light of wood fire and chandelier, was the portrait of the mother of my host, a gracious old lady, dead long ago in a Germany known for its Gemütlichkeit.

We sat at the polished table and drank a gentle hock. The little professor's wife had retired for the night; there was nobody else in the house except the servants, and they were asleep in their attics. Little Max was the typical German musician of the period, his long hair brushed back over a large brow, tiny lenses in his spectacles, a ragged moustache, a gnome of a man brimming with nature and naïve enthusiasm for his art. He was professor of piano at the college of music in Manchester; and the principal and presiding genius of the establishment was Dr. Adolf Brodsky, the first to play the Tchaikovsky Violin Concerto. Long years of residence in Manchester lent neither to Max nor to Adolf the accents of our language; as much German as English was spoken in these homes in Victoria Park, and nearly all the music heard in them was German, though Max favoured Grieg, whom he knew and tried to resemble in appearance.

Outside I heard the wind in the trees. I remembered that when a boy I had got up early on autumn mornings after a gale in the night to go out before nine o'clock school to look with other boys for fuel for November the Fifth. It was in Victoria Park we would search for our most substantial hauls, great snapped-off branches; and we would drag them through the streets and store them for the bonfire night. As silence fell on our conversation in Max's dining-room, I heard the creaking of branches outside. A log in the fire collapsed and the flames and sparks renewed heat and glow, and they were reflected in another portrait, this one over the fireplace—Max's father, and Max was so much like him now that it might easily have been himself. Dead, too, like his mother. And Max had no children.

He spoke of his art as it is seldom spoken of nowadays. Performance was then a means to an end, the making of music. It was a natural part of intercourse between friends, not a public and abnormal achievement. 'Last night Brodsky vos here,' said Max; 'and we play the G major Brahms Sonate; we bofe play it vonce before Brahms himself. And when we haf played, Brodsky he sits down, choost a little 'ot and short of breath; then he stand up immediate, and he says, "Noch einmal, Max;" again we play it, *now*, it is so lofely!' He laughed until tears compelled him to take off his spectacles and wipe them. 'More wine?' he said.

Suddenly I felt the pathos of the scene and the hour. The warm hearth, the portraits on the wall and the sleepers upstairs, the delicate stems of the wine-glasses, the gleam of the oranges on the sideboard; all so tangible and corporeal at this moment of enjoyment. But it was passing; I could hear and feel it vanishing, vanishing now, for all my absorption in the physical as well as the æsthetic reality.

At last I have to go. Max is obviously getting tired. He helps me into my overcoat in the hall, and talks of a cab, but I prefer to walk. He shakes my hand with both of his. As I walk down the drive, I hear him chaining and locking the door. Through the rhododendrons I can see a solitary statue dim but gleaming in the night. . . . For all the years afterwards my supper with Max, at the end of a Hallé Concert, has crystallised for me a set of emotions and sensibilities from which to find an attitude to life, with the mind clarifying opacities of far-off experiences felt and seen. As I look back on this evening a whole world of removed beauty is recalled just for a moment of time.

The houses in Victoria Park are to-day mostly nursing-homes. A tramway clangs through the main thoroughfare; the toll-gates have long since been democratically abolished. No small boys go there early on autumn mornings, looking for wood for the burning of Guy Fawkes, broken branches after the gale in the night.

APPENDIX 2

TOWN CLERK'S REPORT TO THE GENERAL AND PARLIAMENTARY COMMITTEE

/Subject: MANCHESTER CORPORATION BILL, 1954: STREETS IN VICTORIA PARK: VICTORIA PARK TRUST

1. Before the War there were discussions between representatives of the Victoria Park Trust and the Corporation about the condition of the streets in the Park and it was suggested to the Corporation that the protective provisions relating to streets in the Park which are contained in the Corporation's local Acts of Parliament should be repealed so that the streets in the Park might be fully dedicated to the public and be made up and completed, on the understanding however:

    (a) that the Corporation would bear responsibility for the cost of putting the sewerage system into a reasonably satisfactory condition: and

    (b) that the owners of the property in Victoria Park would be responsible in the same way as any owner of property abutting on a private street for the cost of making up and completing the streets.

2. Those discussions were inconclusive but the Trustees have again approached the Corporation. This further approach was reported to the General and Parliamentary Committee on the 22nd October when the Town Clerk pointed out that it would be necessary for the Corporation to decide upon what terms they would be willing to take over responsibility for the streets and sewers in Victoria Park. He also said that before the streets in the Park—other than Anson Road—could be made up and completed at the expense of the frontagers in the normal way it would be necessary to secure the repeal of the restrictive provisions contained in the Corporation's local Acts.

3. The General and Parliamentary Committee then decided, and the Council agreed, that discussions with the Trust should continue

and that in the meantime provisions to the following effect should be inserted in the Bill:

(i) to repeal the protective provisions relating to Victoria Park in the Local Acts of Parliament;

(ii) to provide that the roads—other than Anson Road—in the Park should be deemed to be private streets and the adjoining owners liable to pay private street works expenses.

Provisions on these lines are now included in Clause 75 of the Bill.

4. Further discussions have since taken place with representatives of the Victoria Park Trust as a result of which the following proposals are submitted for the consideration of the Corporation with the intention that they should take effect on the passing of Clause 75 into law:

(a) the following *annual* payments made by the Corporation to the Trust should cease—

(i) the sum of £800 a year in respect of Anson Road being freed from tolls, and

(ii) the sum of £100 a year for the privilege of running tram-cars and Corporation vehicles along Anson Road.

(b) The owners of property in the Park should be liable for the paving of the unmade streets in the same way and subject to the same conditions as applies to other unmade streets in the City:

(c) the Corporation should not make any charge for the reconstruction of the sewers in those streets; the sewers have been in existence for one hundred years and were provided at the cost of the owners or their predecessors in title;

(d) the Corporation should be entitled to remove all posts, barriers, and other obstructions at present existing in streets;

(e) the Corporation should remove and dispose of the toll collectors' huts which have been erected and carry out any necessary consequential reinstatement;

(f) the Corporation should agree to sweep the streets in the Park—but not the back passages—before the streets are made up and completed;

(g) the Trust should transfer to the Corporation any funds or other assets in the hands of the Trust, including books, papers and documents relating to streets and passages in Victoria Park or to the use thereof;

(h) the Corporation should agree to terminate the tenancies of land or buildings held by the Trust for the purposes of the repair of the streets, and

(i) the Corporation should take over such of the workmen

employed on or in connection with the use and repair of streets in the Park as they may decide and discharge those not required. The Corporation should agree to the Trust making some small payment to all or any of the workmen.

5. These proposals have been submitted to the Chairman and Deputy Chairman of the General and Parliamentary Committee and of the Highways Committee, who, after conferring together, have reached the conclusion that subject to an additional provision the proposals embody a fair and reasonable settlement of a most difficult problem. The additional provision suggested is to the effect that pending the paving of the streets in the Park under these arrangements the Corporation should have the right to execute at the expense of the frontagers temporary repairs for patching up the streets.

APPENDIX 3

PROMINENT RESIDENTS OF THE PARK

Name of Resident	Name of house, if any (including any known alternative names)	Address; or site of demolished house	Years residence*	Notes re resident
George Hadfield	1. Hopeville/Thornbury House/Brookfield Hotel	Oxford Place	1837–44	1787–1879. Liberal MP Sheffield 1852–1874; Solicitor from 1810.
	2. (Unnamed)	(No. 2) Conyngham Road	1845–79	
Richard Lane	Park Villa/Victoria Villa/Oxford Villa/Hulme Hall (demolished)	S.W. corner of Oxford Place and Lower Park Road	1838–42	Founder and 1st president Manchester Society of Architects. Architect of Salford Town Hall, Friends Meeting House, Manchester, Chorlton Town Hall (C. on M.), Stockport Infirmary, etc. Founder of Victoria Park.
Edward Riley Langworthy	The Roundwood (demolished) Langdale/Langdale Hall	S.E. corner of Park Crescent. Corner of Upper Park Road and Denison Road	1838–46 1846–74	MP for Salford. Mayor of Salford 1848–50.
Robert Barbour	Ashburne House/Ashburne Hall/Egerton Hall (demolished)	Corner of Oxford Place and Conyngham Road	1841–61	Closely associated with Langworthy in refoundation of Grammar School in 1850s.
James Kershaw	Oaklands/Hulme Hall (demolished)	Opp. Woodthorpe (St. Gabriel's), Oxford Place	1844–58	1795–1864. Liberal MP for Stockport 1847–59; Mayor of Manchester 1842–43.
William Romaine Callender (snr.)	Hopeville/Brookfield Hotel	Oxford Place	1845–64	1794–1864. One of the first Aldermen of the City.
Richard Cobden	Westerfield (demolished)	S.E. corner of Park Crescent	1845–48	1804–65. Member of Parliament, and leading national political figure.

PROMINENT RESIDENTS OF THE PARK

Name of Resident	Name of house, if any (including any known alternative names)	Address; or site of demolished house	Years of residence*	Notes re resident
Charles Hallé	(unnamed)	3 Addison Terrace, Daisy Bank Road	Sept. 1848 (at £12 monthly, furnished)	German-born musician and internationally famous teacher of music.
Lt.-Col. Sir Harry Smith	Summerville (Unitarian College)	Daisy Bank Road	1857–58	1787–1860. South African towns of Ladysmith and Harrismith named after his wife and himself.
William Kessler	Summerville	Daisy Bank Road	1859–1904	Merchant.
William Romaine Callender (jnr.)	Ashburne House/Ashburne Hall/Egerton Hall (demolished)	S.W. corner of Oxford Place and Conyngham Road	1862–71	Merchant. Tory MP for Manchester 1874–76.
Edward Donner	1. (Unnamed)	7 Buckingham Crescent Daisy Bank Road	1863–73	1840–1934. Merchant, politician, and educationalist.
	2. (Unnamed)	No. 4 Anson Road	1873–88	
Sir Henry Enfield Roscoe	1. Hawthornden	S.E. corner of Park Crescent	1864–70	1833–1915. Liberal MP for Manchester South 1885–95; knighted in 1884 for services to technical education
	2. Regent House/Marylands	Lower Park Road	1871–87	
George Beatson Blair	Gladville/Manchester Foot Hospital (N. end)	Anson Road	1864–c. 71	Born 1860; donor of large and important collection of works of art to the City of Manchester; lived in Victoria Park as a boy.
Robert Dukinfield Darbishire	High Elms	Upper Park Road	1867–95	1826–1908. Associated with foundation of Owens College, Manchester High School for Girls, and Whitworth Gallery.
John Slagg	1. The Lodge (demolished)	Oxford Place (1st house on left from Wilmslow Road)	1855–61	1841–89. John Slagg, MP for Manchester 1880–85, lived here with his

Name of Resident	Name of house, if any (including any known alternative names)	Address; or site of demolished house	Years of residence*	Notes re resident
	2. Woodthorpe (demolished)	(2nd house)	1862–74	parents in his youth, and as a young man.
Frederick Melland	(Unnamed) (demolished)	N.E. corner of Park Crescent	1873–95... (1901)–(1911)	Doctor. Daughter (Helen) married Rt. Hon. H. H. Asquith, Prime Minister from 1908 to 1916.
Selmar Nordlinger	1. Olga Villa (demolished)	Anson Road (opp. Milverton Lodge, across Hope Road)	1873–76	Merchant. His daughter Marie was a friend of Marcel Proust, a disciple of Ruskin, and of great help to Proust in his translation of Ruskin's works.*
	2. Gladville/Manchester Foot Hospital (N. end)	Anson Road	1877–89	
Henry Patteson	Elmfield (demolished)	Adjoining Olga Villa, Anson Road	1874–88	Mayor of Manchester 1879–80.
Charles Sacre	Sunnyside	Conyngham Road	1875–89	Chief Mechanical Engineer, Manchester, Sheffield & Lincolnshire Railway.
Thomas Sowler	Oak Bank/Hulme Hall (demolished)	Opp. Woodthorpe, Oxford Place	1877–91	1818–91. Succeeded father as publisher of Manchester Courier in 1871; published Evening Mail in 1874. Parliamentary candidate in 1885.
Ford Madox Brown	(Unnamed)	3 Addison Terrace, Daisy Bank Road	1883–87	Artist. Painted murals in Large Hall of Manchester Town Hall.
Edward Solomons	The Gables	Hope Road, Anson Road	1885–91	Architect of Reform Club, Prince's Theatre, Manchester & Salford Savings Bank office, warehouses and private dwellings.
Rose Hyland	1. Arden Lea	Almost opp. 'Graham', Dalton Hall, Conyngham Road.	1885–91	Suffragette—closely associated with Pankhursts.
	2. Holly Bank	Oxford Place	1891–95 (1901)–(1911)	

* Marie Nordlinger [Mrs Riefstal] published 41 of Proust's letters to her (1899-1908) in M. Proust, *Lettres à une amie*, Manchester, 1942.

PROMINENT RESIDENTS OF THE PARK

Name of Resident	Name of house, if any (including any known alternative names)	Address; or site of demolished house	Years of residence*	Notes re resident
Arthur Macdonald Blair	The Lodge	Oxford Place (1st house on left from Wilmslow Rd.)	1886–89	Manchester Solicitor.
Wm. Gaddum	1. Garbness/Toc H Mk IV	Upper Park Road	1886–88	East India Merchant.
	2. Stoneywood/Saville House/ Ward Hall	Lower Park Road	1889–95	
Arthur Schuster	1. (Unnamed)	No. 4 Anson Road	1889–95	Professor of Applied Maths, 1881, Professor of Physics 1888, Manchester University.
	2. Kent House/St. Anselm Hall	Kent Road East	1895–(1911)	
Richard Marsden Pankhurst	(Unnamed)	4 Buckingham Crescent, Daisy Bank Road	1894–98	His wife and daughters were leading suffragettes.
Elias Bancroft	(Unnamed)	7 Buckingham Crescent, Daisy Bank Road	1893–(1901)	d. 1924. Artist; for many years Hon. Secretary of Manchester Academy of Fine Arts.
Sheridan Delepine	1. Schoenkamp (demolished)	Anson Road (S.E. corner of junction with Upper Kent Road)	1894–	Professor of Pathology until 1904 and of Comparative Pathology and Bacteriology from 1904 at Manchester University; founder of Public Health Laboratory.
	2. Dalton House/Eaglesfield	Opp. Milverton Lodge, Anson Road	–(1901)–	
Gerald B. Hertz (later Hurst)	1. Elmhurst	2 Buckingham Cresent, Daisy Bank Road	1905–11	1877–1957, Barrister, Conservative politician, historian. Knighted 1929.
	2. Unnamed			

*From entries in Rusholme Rate Books; bracketed dates are from later directories.

INDEX